THE QUALITY MOVEMENT

What Total Quality Management is Really All About!

Helga Drummond

Kogan Page, London / Nichols Publishing New Jersey

Dedication

To Finestone
for your prayers.

First published in 1992

Apart from any fair dealing for the purposes of research or private study, or criticism or review, as permitted under the Copyright, Designs and Patents Act, 1988, this publication may only be reproduced, stored or transmitted, in any form or by any means, with the prior permission in writing of the publishers, or in the case of reprographic reproduction in accordance with the terms of licences issued by the Copyright Licensing Agency. Enquiries concerning reproduction outside those terms should be sent to the publishers at the undermentioned address:

Kogan Page Limited
120 Pentonville Road
London N1 9JN

© Helga Drummond, 1992

British Library Cataloguing in Publication Data
A CIP record for this book is available from the British Library.

ISBN 0 7494 0753 0

Published in the United States of America by Nichols Publishing, P.O. Box 6036, East Brunswick, New Jersey 08816

A CIP record for this book is available from the Library of Congress.

ISBN 0 89397 383 1

Typeset by BookEns Limited, Baldock, Herts
Printed in England by Clays Ltd., St Ives plc.

CONTENTS

ACKNOWLEDGEMENTS

I first learned of the existence of the quality movement from Elizabeth Chell. I am grateful for our many discussions about the managerial implications of TQM which helped to shape the ideas contained in this book. I also thank my colleagues at the Institute of Public Administration and Management – Morton Davies, Colin Murray, Chris Pycroft and David Watt, for the opportunity to rehearse part of the material in staff meetings. The clarity of my thinking was much improved at the expense of detaining everyone an hour longer.

Liverpool University,
June, 1992.

PREFACE

In the summer of 1962, aged six, I journeyed from Edinburgh to Sheffield with my mother and brother. As the train reversed out of Leeds city station, I saw beneath the viaduct, a huge concentration of back-to-back houses. I had never seen anything like it before, row upon row of grey slates, dull red brick, and, most disturbing, washing hanging across the street. I remember thinking how I would hate to live anywhere like that.

Life is a long irony. I went to university in Leeds, and for the first three summers of my working life lived amidst back-to-backs, washing pegged out across the street. My first job was in a small clothing factory known as William Pell & Co in East Street, ten minutes' walk away. The postcard in the Job Centre had indicated that a production assistant was required: 'Some clerical work now, more later.'

Jack Newton, the production manager, explained the actual duties in a word: ''umpin', ie moving mountains of baskets of partially completed suitings from one machinist to another. My induction was equally laconic: 'You see those women down there,' said Jack Newton, 'they're evil.'

'Evil' was not a term I had encountered in undergraduate management textbooks. Besides, I soon discovered that as far as the workforce were concerned, the forces of darkness resided in the managing director's office, in that individual's overriding concern for production. I was assured that under Mr Black, the previous owner, 'It were a lovely shop. There used to be singing in those days. Now there's a clock hanging from the ceiling.'

I could understand the managing director's point of view, however. When I arrived, there were approximately 100 employees producing around 100 suits per week. The average wage was about

£35 per week and the suits were sold for £45 each. Even allowing for overheads, cost of materials, discounts and bad debts, in 1977 the place yielded a reasonable surplus. If, however, production could be increased to 120 or more suits per week, then the margin would be handsome indeed – hence the intensive time study and the concomitant disinclination to sing about it.

My first introduction to quality was the prospect of a large order from Marks and Spencer – subject to inspection. This was good business if it could be won. Accordingly, the stairs were scrubbed, special sandwiches ordered, and the staff carefully briefed: 'No smoking, no swearing, no farting – till they've gone.'

Then, a graduate on the shop floor was a rarity, and I attracted the attention of a man I knew only as Finestone. Finestone's job was to hand-sew the braid on the collars, lapels and trousers of dinner suits. I can still visualise him, small, dark, perched stoop-shouldered on a high stool, peering over his glasses whenever the 'bawling and shouting' erupted. 'Your education is marvellous' he said every time I paused by his workbench. Finestone had once owned an exclusive costumier's in Leeds, with the emphasis on 'exclusive'. The height of his career had been when he tailored a costume for the Princess Royal at Harewood. He received a letter of thanks from her lady-in-waiting and was much moved by it. He kept a roll of his 'exclusive' labels beside him and one day, cut one for me. The label bore the name 'Finestone' in brown copperplate lettering on a background of gold watered silk. I kept it for a long time.

Finestone repeatedly counselled me not to marry a factory worker, because 'he has no money'. Yet for all that, one day as he showed me photographs of himself with his grandchildren in the garden of his home in Alwoodly, Finestone said, 'money is not everything.' There was an edge to his voice and I never knew why. I was twenty-one, he was eighty-four and in the careless days of youth that was just one of the questions I never thought to ask him.

Fifteen years later, as this book was nearing completion, I returned to East End Park. The houses were still the same. The washing was still strung across the streets and the black satanic-looking church still dominated the landscape. The factory was gone, the site neatly flattened to rubble. Curiously enough, the steps had survived – the same steps which I had mounted clutching my Job Centre card, and which had been scrubbed in Marks and Spencer's honour. I did not stay long. It was a Sunday afternoon, the area was deserted, and there was a chill wind blowing from the north east. Besides, what was there to see in an empty space? Then I remembered it had once known the sound of voices singing.

INTRODUCTION

Quality has emerged as the managerial imperative of the decade. It is virtually impossible to open a professional or trade journal without seeing some slogan such as 'quality counts', or 'right first time'.

Yet despite all the hype and publicity, it is difficult to discover what the quality movement is all about. Although there are many books on various aspects of quality, none supplies a panoramic overview. The first purpose of this book is to fill that gap by providing a resumé of the major themes of the quality movement, in one short, simple, and, I hope, readable volume.

The second purpose in writing is to explore some of the implications of quality for management. There is considerably more to the production of quality goods and services than 'doing the job correctly', or satisfying an audit, important though these objectives may be. Building a quality culture involves a fundamental transformation of organisations and of the nature of work and employment. Management as we know it will be swept away in what is already being called 'the new industrial revolution'. As to what will follow, who knows?

1

THE QUALITY MOVEMENT

On the eighth day of May [1382], . . . [five citizens] came before the Mayor, sheriffs and aldermen . . . and showed to them two pieces of cooked fish . . . rotten and stinking and unwholesome . . . which they had bought of John Welburgham . . . at noon on the same day and which the said cook warranted to them to be good . . . .

And hereupon the said John Welburgham was immediately sent for, and, being questioned, he said that he did sell . . . the said fish to be cooked . . . . Wherefore it was awarded that the said John Welburgham should repay to said complainant six pence, . . . that he should also have the punishment of the pillory for one hour of the day, and that the said fish should then be burned beneath him.[1]

In medieval times, quality was a serious issue. In the case described above the whole town becomes involved as the miscreant is summoned, tried and sentenced that same day. Moreover not only is the said John Welburgham required to compensate his victims, but he must also endure public humiliation including the ritualistic destruction of his rotten goods.

THE ORIGINS OF THE QUALITY MOVEMENT

The medieval obsession with quality may be explained by the scarcity of resources. Then, starvation was a real possibility. Consumer goods, being handcrafted, were extremely expensive. Thirteen quires of paper, for example, cost six shillings and eight pence, as against a penny for ten eggs and fourpence for a best roast hen.[2] One bad quire therefore represented a considerable loss, let alone the whole consignment proving unsatisfactory.

Nowadays we are all victims of quality failures daily, such as late trains, leaking car-door seals and prematurely expiring light bulbs. The loss is invariably borne by the consumer, as the real costs of a quality failure are often out of all proportion to the value of the defective item. For instance, a car may be repaired under warranty, but where is the compensation for being stranded miles from a telephone in pitch darkness and freezing rain? Likewise, what comfort is a quid knocked off a restaurant bill when the occasion has been a social disaster? Besides, recompense is by no means automatic, especially where larger sums of money are involved. Obtaining redress through the courts is a tortuous experience; even if a favourable judgement is obtained, it seldom mitigates the total loss.

History is repeating itself, however, as customers are becoming increasingly intolerant of poor service, late deliveries, unreliable goods, shoddy workmanship and the like. The examples of excellence set by a few organisations leave the rest looking distinctly shabby. Deprived of the psychological satisfaction of pillorying suppliers, consumers are nevertheless exerting control by taking their custom elsewhere. The results of this new-found preference for virtue were first seen in the car industry, as Japanese manufacturers' reputation for reliability and value for money began, and continues, to seriously undermine their Western competitors. The so-called 'Citizens' Charter' has added further impetus to the improvement of quality.

QUALITY AS THE NEW COMPETITIVE WEAPON

Organisations everywhere are growing increasingly conscious of the competitive potential of quality. Even such a hallowed English institution as the Bar is beginning to perceive the value of responding to clients' needs. For instance, some provincial chambers have taken the trouble to streamline their procedures and so have reduced waiting lists to a quarter of the length of those in London. Consequently even the most prestigious London sets have lost clients.

Many public services must now compete for work in a way unimaginable 10 or 15 years ago. Quality has become an issue because standards are now contractually defined, whereas previously they were vague and unmonitored. In the health and education sectors, institutions now vie with one another for custom.

Rivalry focuses not on price but quality. Universities, for example, are ranked according to reserach output, with leading establishments being awarded a disproportionately high share of funds, while the future of those with poor ratings is bleak. Such is the economic and political climate that ever-higher standards are demanded in the face of diminished and diminishing resources.

WHAT IS TOTAL QUALITY MANAGEMENT?

Total quality management, referred to hereafter as TQM, is basically a business philosophy founded on customer satisfaction:

> The business process starts with the customer. In fact if it is not started with the customer, it all too often abruptly ends with the customer.[3]

Although a new customer consciousness is evident in many organisations, TQM involves more than wishing customers a nice day and providing free newspapers for hotel guests. Welcome though these improvements may be, they are often superficial, concerned more with appearance than with any deep commitment to customer satisfaction. A complimentary newspaper, for example, is of little use to the hotel guest turned away at reception because his room has been double-booked. Likewise, the customer who collects his sleeping bag from the dry cleaners to discover that it has all but dissolved is hardly going to be impressed by uniforms and name-badges.

TQM involves designing organisations to please customers day in day out. It has two strands, namely:

1. Careful design of the product or service.

2. Ensuring that the organisation's systems can consistently produce the design.[4]

Those twin objectives can only be achieved if the whole organisation is orientated towards them – hence the term 'total' quality management. Orientating the organisation to quality requires more, much more, than a managerial proclamation that from tomorrow everything will be different.

Developing TQM is like planting a garden.

To begin with, you cannot throw money at it. Not even a million-aire can telephone and order a garden for delivery by nine o'clock tomorrow morning. Creating a garden requires vision, planning, and the disciplined application of skill and effort. Success favours the patient and the conscientious. The same applies to TQM; it cannot be bought and installed like a piece of computer software. It too must be planned, the ground prepared etc, and, like planting a garden, it takes time. Organisations which have begun to implement TQM find that it takes at least two to three years to begin to reap the fruits of change.

What is quality?

Although some products and services may have a magical quality about them, quality is rarely the result of magic. Output is strictly a function of input. The cook who takes a pork chop and pours a tin of tomato soup over it, produces a dish which looks and tastes like a pork chop with a tin of tomato soup poured over it, no matter what exotic name he gives it. The greengrocer whose produce is always sparkling fresh owes his success not to witchcraft, but to going to the market every day, unlike other greengrocers who may only go twice a week.

Quality must be worked at and consciously achieved. Although organisations only get out of their production systems what they put into them, efforts must be carefully directed if the results are to be satisfactory. If the greengrocer's assistants damage the produce by careless handling, for example, his trips to the market will have been wasted. Quality management demands attention to the whole of the transformation system, ie:

- The quality and suitability of inputs.
- The manner in which inputs are delivered, stored, and transformed into a product or service.
- The manner in which the product or service is delivered to the customer, used and installed.

Like a garden, TQM is never finished. Continuous improvement is a fundamental tenet of TQM philosophy.

The proverb teaches that when the house is finished, death enters in. Standards either rise or they fall. Sometimes they fall because complacency and/or greed supervene. Sometimes the decline is relative, as competitors reach new levels of achievement. Survival demands constant attention and responsiveness to customers.[5]

THE COSTS OF QUALITY

Quality is often associated with expense. We expect to pay more for a gold-nibbed fountain pen, for example, than for a pen fitted with a steel nib. A five-star hotel is considerably more expensive than a private guest house. Even when comparing like with like, consumers are often willing to pay for better quality. The retail chain Marks and Spencer, for instance, is renowned for quality goods and premium prices.

What pleases a customer most, however, is superior quality for the same money or, better still, for less money. Herein lies the success of the Japanese car manufacturers, small brewers of real ale, and back street garages, to name but a few instances of proof that *quality goods and services cost less to produce, not more.*

The rationale for this assertion is explained elsewhere in this book. Here, it is sufficient to note that TQM results in cost reductions through:

- reduced waste;
- greater productivity;
- increased sales.

These three factors are interactive. TQM begins with a comprehensive analysis of existing systems and procedures which identifies waste and suggests possibilities for speeding up operations. Improving systems reduces the scrap and rework and improves reliability, thus making the product or service more attractive. Increased sales facilitate price reductions which further enhance appeal, and so it goes on.

BEYOND QUALITY

Quality is a means to an end.

The end is continued viability. Organisations will increasingly find themselves competing not on one front, but four, namely:

1. Quality.

2. Cost.

3. Flexibility.

4. Delivery.

Having achieved a significant lead in quality, the Japanese are now turning their attention to cost. Although many Japanese products are already competitive both in terms of quality and price, the aim is to seek further and more drastic cost reductions, by eliminating waste.[6] Waste means non-value-adding activities. For example, the only thing of value to someone engaging a window cleaner is a clean window. Activities such as filling the bucket with water, squeezing the sponge, hoisting the ladders and climbing them add cost but no value. Moreover, the longer these operations take, the more expensive the service becomes. The Japanese have achieved some spectacular results in reducing non-productive activities. Some manufacturing set-up times, for example, have been cut from five hours to three minutes.[7] Pause for a moment and consider the magnitude of this reduction. Imagine it being repeated for 10 or 15 operations – what possibilities might that create? Such improvements result from challenging assumptions about what is the most cost-effective mode of operation. Conventional mass production, far from generating economies of scale, can be extremely wasteful. So can taken-for-granted practices. Is it, for instance, necessary to *drill* a hole, or will it suffice to cut around the circumference? This might seem a trivial question, but if the operation is one which is repeated many thousands of times then the potential for saving time and money may be considerable.

Achievement in one area opens up possibilities in others. Reduction in set-up times enables manufacturers to extend the range of choice to customers, as they can switch more easily from one product to another, thus adding another dimension to competition. Further, fast flexible production means shortened delivery times. The minimum Western time-scale for delivery of cars from factory to customer is eight weeks. In Japan it is nearer two weeks.

'WHAT WORKS IN JAPAN WON'T WORK HERE'

Japan's success is sometimes attributed to cultural differences. The stereotype is one of workers willing to work very long hours and to subordinate themselves absolutely to the organisation. These supposed virtues are contrasted unfavourably with the stereotypical idle, unco-operative and dense British worker. For example:

> As British's industrialists were urging one another to lead the charge to recovery, two British Rail workmen on Greenwich station were shovelling debris into a motorised cart on caterpillar tracks. 'Better than a wheelbarrow,' observed a waiting passenger. 'Must hold three times as much.'
>
> By the time the train was due, the cart was full. One workman rested, while the other started it up and steered it at a snail's pace up the platform which is separated by a railing from a strip of grass. 'But much slower than a wheelbarrow,' the passenger added, 'though it must cost a dozen times more.'
>
> As the train arrived, five minutes late, the workman was inching down the ramp at the platform's end. And by the time the train pulled out, he was edging up the ramp to the strip on the other side of the railing.
>
> 'Blimey, they're going to dump it on the grass,' said the passenger. 'They don't even need a wheelbarrow – they could just shovel the stuff straight over the fence.'[8]

Quite apart from the fact that it is the management who are responsible for working practices, both stereotypes are misleading. Indeed, anecdotal evidence suggests that leading Japanese firms prefer British workers to Japanese workers, precisely because the former are more questioning and show greater initiative!

Building a quality culture has nothing to do with turning workers into kamikaze squads. It is about creating an organisational infrastructure consistent with continuous improvement. The task is by no means as easy as much of the current managerial rhetoric might suggest. Part of the problem is the duality of TQM philosophy, which stresses both the instrumental and the inspirational. The procedural aspects of TQM can defeat their own objective. Conversely the dream culture espoused by Peters and Waterman is like the biblical seed scattered on shallow ground – the initial flush of enthusiasm soon withers because there is nothing to sustain it.

TQM requires a second-order change.

Instead of change within the system, it is the system itself which must be changed. Building a quality culture involves reversing fundamental assumptions about managing organisations. *The first of these assumptions which must be reversed is the concern for short-term profits.*

Whereas organisations have hitherto been orientated to a profit culture, the TQM imperative is customer satisfaction. The argument is that if organisations pay sufficient attention to quality, profits will follow, whereas if they concern themselves solely with profits, they will bankrupt themselves.

In the short term, TQM will demand far higher standards of management than are currently considered acceptable. For example, a recent television programme about a factory trying to introduce 'JIT' (Just in Time) production showed management promising to supply new machinery in return for trade union co-operation. Such behaviour is outrageous. Machines should be replaced as necessary, not traded as bargaining counters. Further, it will no longer be good enough (if it ever was) to instruct supervisors and staff to 'work round problems'. TQM requires managers to pro-duce solutions instead of merely demanding results.

In the longer term it is foreseeable that managers as we know them will become redundant. Leaders will be necessary to inspire and nurture development. However, their terms of reference are likely to be radically different from today's managers. Indeed, the whole structure of employment will need to be transformed if organisations are to free themselves from the vestiges of the profit culture.

BEATING THE JAPANESE

Despite their impressive achievements, *the Japanese are not infallible.* New car designs, for instance, are still announced upon what are believed to be lucky days.[9] Despite Taguchi's contribution to design theory (see Chapter 3) it is reported that Hitachi budgeted $1,000,000 to steal the design specifications of IBM's 3081 com-puter.[10]

It will be argued that the Achilles' heel of Japanese industry is its reliance upon coercion.[11] The race is by no means run and it is questionable whether the Japanese system can withstand the stresses of force indefinitely. Indeed, it may already be crumbling; according to some accounts *one Japanese worker commits suicide every twenty minutes*, such is the pressure to perform. Even if this statistic is but a shadow of the truth, it nevertheless suggests there is something badly wrong. There is an alternative; the future ultimately belongs to the organisations which grasp it.

SUMMARY

- Customers everywhere are becoming increasingly intolerant of poor goods and services.
- Quality is a formidable competitive weapon.
- TQM is a business philosophy based upon customer satisfaction.
- TQM consists of two strands, ie:

    — quality of design;
    — quality of conformance to design.

- TQM cannot be purchased and installed like a piece of computer software; implementation is like planting a garden.
- Quality is the result of inputs and efforts and the manner in which these are utilised.
- TQM requires continuous improvement.
- Quality reduces cost through:

    — reduced waste;
    — greater productivity;
    — increased sales.

- Quality is a means to an end.
- Competition has gone beyond quality to include cost, customer choice, and delivery time.
- Building a quality culture is not about creating fanatical workforce commitment, but about abandoning outdated business and management assumptions.
- Japanese companies are not infallible. They may yet be overtaken.

2

THE DEMING PHILOSOPHY

Edward Deming must have a strange horoscope. When he was born the fairies might have said:

You will become famous, but not until you are a very old man. Ignored in the West, your star shall rise in the East and then the whole world shall listen.

In the 1950s American industry was enjoying a boom. Whatever could be made could be sold. The future looked certain to remain prosperous. Few industrialists heeded the work of this man called Deming and his ideas about quality, and his new-fangled statistics. In Japan, however, things were very different. The Japanese economy was depressed, goods stamped 'Made in Japan' were renowned for high price and poor quality.

Japanese industrialists were receptive to Deming's ideas and set about implementing them. By the mid-1970s, Japan was beginning to seriously undermine its American and other Western competitors, first in cars and then in a whole range of goods including videos, hi-fi, and computers. Then and only then, did Western industrialists begin to take Deming seriously.

THE DEMING PHILOSOPHY

Deming's approach to quality is set out in his so-called 'Fourteen Points' of management.[1] Each of these is described in detail later in this chapter. Here it is sufficient to say that Deming's philosophy is founded upon three basic precepts. They are:

1. Customer orientation.

2. Continuous improvement.

3.   Quality is determined by the system.

The full meaning and implications of these ideas will emerge as this chapter proceeds. Briefly, Deming's argument is that competitiveness depends upon customer satisfaction. Customer satisfaction is created through a combination of responsiveness to the customer's views and needs, and continuous improvement of products or services. Quality is a fundamental customer requirement. It is determined not by exhorting people to work harder or threatening them with the sack or humiliation, but by the system. The system is defined as inputs, and the manner in which these are processed.

Point 1: 'Create constancy of purpose for improvement of product and service'

Deming argues that *the aim of continuous improvement should be reflected in all aspects of an organisation's strategy.*

Continuous improvement means just what it says. In order to remain competitive, organisations must constantly seek ways of improving their production systems and the customer appeal of their products. Improvement is not merely the responsibility of production and sales department, it must be the aim:

■   in all operations;
■   at all levels;
■   in all plans, short-, medium- and long-term.

According to Deming, organisations are influenced too greatly by opportunism and short-term priorities, instead of ensuring that their business will be viable a decade hence. Organisations which twist and change direction in response to every fluctuation in the market and every perceived new opening cannot cultivate the competency which is the foundation of excellence – sticking to the knitting, as Peters and Waterman put it.[2] Business history is rich in examples of disastrous moves into unfamiliar terrain – for example, Prudential's dramatic entry into the estate agency business in the late 1980s, and their equally dramatic exit. It is only sensible to seize opportunities if the capability exists to exploit these, but capability takes time to develop, if indeed it can be developed at all. To use the garden analogy, carrots require sandy soil. If the soil is heavy clay base, then the gardener must think again, however tempting the price of carrots. For example:

> The management of a company that makes furniture, doing well, took it into their heads to expand their line into pianos. Why not make pianos? They bought a Steinway piano, took it apart, made or bought parts, and put a piano together exactly like the Steinway, only to discover that they could only get thuds out of their product. So they put the Steinway piano back together with the intention to get their money back on it, only to discover that it too would now only make thuds.[3]

Improving quality: where to start

Deming recommends beginning with a comprehensive and systematic appraisal of the business including its:

- products;
- methods of production;
- materials requirements;
- marketing strategy;
- training and education.

Above all, Deming urges organisations to keep their attention focused upon the customer rather than the competition. Competition, says Deming, will always be there. Today it is Japan, tomorrow it will be elsewhere in the Far East.[4] According to Deming, if customer satisfaction is maintained, competitors are irrelevant.

Point 2: 'Adopt the new philosophy'

When we fit a new electric light bulb and find that it works, we are relieved. We willingly spend an extra £200 on second-year warranty for a new car because we believe that the probability of something expensive going wrong is high. We pay more to buy a personal computer from a shop rather than through mail order, just in case it happens to break down. In short, we have become conditioned to expect a proportion of 'duds' in manufactured goods. The same applies to services, except that our expectations are even lower. When did the morning train last run on time? How often do you receive letters delivered to the wrong address? A good package holiday is something that gets talked about on the radio!

Organisations perpetuate these expectations, as anyone confronted with malfunctioning electronics in a new car will know. The garage will allow the customer to go to court rather than replace the vehicle or refund the money. Usually it never comes to that, as customers are fobbed off with excuses such as 'We have to get in touch with the manufacturer'; or 'It's a design fault' (which it probably is), or are worn down by trouble and expense as repeated visits to the workshop prove unsuccessful.

Of course many companies pride themselves upon the efficiency of their complaints departments. If a hair dryer breaks down, for example, they will replace it promptly, no questions asked. They overlook both the cost and the fact that *the customer would rather have a reliable product in the first place*.

In Deming's view, *defects are expensive and unnecessary*. Defects are expensive because they require a whole organisational infrastructure to manage them – factory rework sections, complaints departments, 'returned goods' counters plus all of the administrative work involved all cost money. The costs are ultimately borne by the customer.

In Deming's view, *defects are not inevitable*. To illustrate this point, imagine boiling an egg. Perfection entails placing the egg in a sufficient depth of boiling water and removing it as soon as the sand has run through the egg timer. Is there any reason why a defect, ie egg too hard or too soft, should be inevitable?

Deming argues: *defects are a product of the system*. In the case of the egg, a defect might be caused by inadequate knowledge, insufficient water, an inaccurate timer, power failure, external distraction, or using a rotten egg in the first place. All of these factors are tangibles and are therefore manageable. The same argument applies to even the most complex products and services. Defects are usually traceable to some cause or combination of causes, such as bad design, unsuitable materials, poor tools, machine faults, inadequate training, and so forth.

According to Deming, managerial career structures exacerbate the problem. So called 'fast-tracking', whereby managers expect to be in a job for only two to three years, means they are seldom motivated to tackle problems at source. To do so would be to risk causing upset and so forfeiting a good reference. Moreover, the likelihood of being far away before the consequences of their omissions emerge encourages managers to concentrate upon short-term success.

Another point implied in Deming's philosophy is that *being able to do a good job creates satisfaction*. As Deming notes, producing shoddy goods gives little pleasure. Imagine, for example, the unease of a waiter serving burnt food; the car service receptionist returning a car, knowing that no one has even opened the bonnet, far less changed the oil or checked the brakes. Many good trades- men will not undertake an instruction to 'do a cheap job', as it hurts them too much. They would rather lose the business.

Point 3: 'Cease dependence upon mass inspection'

Deming is not suggesting that inspection be eliminated, but that *reliance* upon inspection is inconsistent with quality. He argues that if inspection is necessary to prevent defects, then the process is incapable of meeting specifications. The crux of Deming's argu- ment is that quality comes not from inspection, but through improving the system.

It is impossible, says Deming, to inspect quality into a product or service; quality must be designed in.

Designing for quality involves every aspect of the organisation and its products or services.

Design in this context means that requirements must be thought through and clearly specified. This applies not just to the main production process, but to all ancillary activities. Hospitals, for example, depend not only upon the quality of their medical and paramedical staff, but on porters, cleaners and even volunteers. The aim of TQM is to ensure that the system delivers what it is intended to deliver,[5] and this begins with design. It is far better, for instance, to devise simple forms than to employ people to inspect for mistakes in complicated ones. Likewise, the better the systems of fare collection on buses and trains, the fewer ticket collectors and inspectors required. (See chapter 3 for a detailed discussion of designing for quality.)

The greater the number of inspectors the greater the number of defects.

The fatigue and boredom of routine inspection is hardly conducive to reliability. Increasing the number of checks only exacerbates the problem. This is because if someone knows that an item has been inspected twice already and must pass five more checks, they will probably give it only a cursory glance. It will be assumed that the product is satisfactory because it has already been checked twice, and besides, if there is a defect, someone further up the line will notice it.

Point 4: 'End the practice of awarding business on the basis of a price tag alone'

Commercial contracts are typically awarded to the lowest bidder. Deming opposes this practice. He argues that it is always possible to drive price down, but that those who do, succeed at the expense of quality, because they only get what they pay for. Pressurising a supplier on price creates the temptation to take short-cuts, preferably where the customer cannot see. Consequently, considerable damage may be done before such deficiencies are detected. *Would you engage a cheap electrician?*

The initial cost of supplies is only one factor in the equation. What counts is the overall cost, and often the overall cost of cheap supplies is high. A cheap insurance policy, for example, may actually prove very expensive when all the exclusions and limitations on amounts payable are taken into account. Likewise, cut-price yarns become extremely expensive if they are prone to breaking during weaving. The cost of machine down-time is likely to far exceed the cost of better-quality materials.

Single-source suppliers

Basing purchasing decisions upon price alone entails frequent changes of supplier. Here is an example of what can happen:

A factory purchased a consignment of cloth for manufacture into high-quality suits. The cloth was inspected by a most experienced production manager before being cut. Once in production however, problems developed. High-quality garments are pressed several times during production. In this instance, no matter how hard the operatives tried, the pieces of material could not be pressed into shape. A few suits were completed to ascertain what the finished product would look like. Shortly afterwards, these worn and baggy-looking garments were scrapped, along with the remaining work in progress.

If you were the manager what would you do: sack the production manager, sue the supplier, or both? The production manager was a skilled and conscientious employee. Analysis showed that the cloth conformed exactly to specifications. The source of the problem remained a mystery, though it illustrates Deming's point that *specifications and performance are not synonymous.*

As with the cloth, supplies may conform exactly to specifications and yet prove unsuitable in production, or mar the finished product. Deming says it is therefore vital that the supplier understands:

- the end use of supplies;
- the manner in which these are processed.

Deming advocates single source, long-term relationships with suppliers, and puts forward several advantages of single sourcing:

Consistency
Materials from different suppliers are never identical, even though they may conform exactly to specifications. Deming argues that the variation inherent in materials from one supplier alone is sufficiently problematic, without compounding the difficulties. Further, competition for single supplier status, as distinct from cut-throat competition on price, is a healthy stimulus to continuous improvement.

Reduced cost
The fewer the suppliers, the lower the administrative costs. Most organisations utilise multi-sourcing in order to avoid late deliveries and stock-outs. According to Deming, however, single sourcing actually reduces the probability of this happening because it makes life more predictable for the supplier, and deepens his knowledge of the vendor's needs because of greater contact between the two. It is better, says Deming, to develop trust and confidence with one supplier than to retain several as a precaution.

The following quotation, which expresses the old Pullman company's attitude towards its suppliers, encapsulates the spirit of Deming's philosophy:

Pullman was a prestige account. Always mindful of that,

unproductive overheads were kept to a minimum. The fewer the accounts the less office work was involved. Accounts were carefully selected, requirements specified, there was loyalty to suppliers and accounts were paid promptly. In return no matter what happened the cars had to be supplied and a continuity of service was as important as the quality and price of the supplies.[6]

Choosing suppliers

Deming suggests choosing suppliers on the basis of their adherence to his 'Fourteen Points', and especially Point Five, which concerns commitment to continuous improvement (see below). The critical factors are a prospective supplier's:

■ past record for product development;
■ commitment of funds to research and development;
■ general quality system.

The first two of these factors are self-explanatory. As regards the third, Deming recommends that purchasers concern themselves not only with how supplies are produced, but also the manner of delivery. How are goods transported? Are the containers clean, well-maintained and suitable for the purpose?

Point 5: 'Improve constantly and forever the system of production'

Continuous improvement means making every new product better than the last. The argument is:

Why not? Why repeat over and over the same mistakes?[7]

There are now signs which suggest improvement concerns more than just avoiding past mistakes.

Continuous improvement is becoming a competitive imperative.

Price-cutting in the airline business, for example, has given way to an emphasis on passenger comfort. So intense is the competition that major innovations and upgradings can become 'old hat' within less than a year. Deming suggests that particular attention should be paid to product design, as this is where the greatest potential for improvement often exists. Quality must be incorporated at the design stage of a product. Once production is under way, it is too late. Since a product cannot exceed the limitations of its design, faults may be irredeemable. For example:

Customer: 'But you promised to fix this toaster to work as good as new!'

Retailer: 'We did.'

Customer: 'But it doesn't work!'

Retailer: 'It didn't work when it was new either.'[8]

Deming argues that quality is not about meeting specifications, but about reducing variability through improving the process and satisfying the customer's needs. This requires a multi-disciplinary approach to design, instead of the traditional practice whereby products are designed in a vacuum and tossed 'over the wall' into production, who do their best with it and then toss it 'over the wall,' into sales.[9]

Point 6: 'Institute training'

Continuous improvement implies heavy and ongoing investment in training. Deming argues that organisations make too many assumptions about what people know and what they can do. In my view, Deming's point is particularly relevant to blue-collar staff. Manual tasks are defined as 'unskilled' and therefore it is assumed that training is unnecessary. For example, a Director of Recreation Services once noted that the floors in all the sports centres were sticky, which made them feel dirty. Middle managers said that problem was due to staff laziness. Dissatisfied with this explanation, the Director consulted a cleaning expert. The expert reported that the problem was caused by staff using too much detergent. Having never been trained, though there are college courses in cleaning techniques, the staff were trying to do a good job by using plenty of detergent. When the results were unsatisfactory they tried to overcome the problem by adding more detergent, unaware that they were only making things worse.

Point 7: 'Adopt and institute leadership'

Deming argues that organisations have become overly concerned with control, at the expense of leadership. Deming argues that managers should devote their energies to making improvements, translating vision into action and acquiring in-depth knowledge about the work they supervise, rather than focusing upon outcomes such as 'management by objectives' and 'zero defects'. Leaders, says Deming, should concentrate upon improving the system rather than seeking to apportion blame to individuals. They should also be able to seek and receive support from higher management in resolving problems.

Point 8: 'Drive out fear'

Deming equates fear with loss. Fear, argues Deming, stems from insecurity, such as being worried about losing one's job or being unable to solve a particular problem or answer a particular question. Insecurity results in loss, because it forces individuals to concentrate upon satisfying rules and playing the system at the expense of making real contributions to the organisation.

Management by fear is a substitute for planning and analysis, and seldom a successful one. The management of a supermarket chain, for instance, were concerned about shrinkage, ie the difference between stock inputs and outputs. Instead of investigating the problem, a decree was issued: 'Shrinkage must not exceed 1 per cent' – or else. And so it came to pass that shrinkage remained within the 1 per cent limit. Yet all that happened was that store managers arranged for a little more fat to be left on the meat, stopped stocking highly perishable though highly popular fruits, etc.[10] Lacking the operational knowledge to anticipate this response, the senior management thought they had brought the problem under control, when in reality the losses were worse than ever, as the customers were now suffering.

Point 9: 'Break down barriers between staff areas'

Deming says that it is essential that people throughout the organisation appreciate one another's problems. Purchasing staff, for example, must understand the importance of consulting with producing managers before changing the supply of raw materials, as the most minute difference can cause enormous variations in manufacture. Such a high level of understanding and commitment to mutual problem-solving requires deep cultural and structural changes. Without such changes, says Deming, training programmes are worthless.

Obviously there will be disagreement between departments. Sales staff, for instance, may resist the idea of zero stocks because of the risk of losing a customer. Deming argues that it is management's responsibility to resolve such conflict in the best interests of the organisation.

Point 10: 'Eliminate slogans, exhortations and targets for the workforce'

Deming views slogans and exhortations as evidence of failure to manage. Deming's argument is that if good systems are installed, including proper staff training and management, then entreaties to work harder and make fewer mistakes are unnecessary. Imagine, for example, an operative being asked to sign a pledge: 'I will hereafter produce no defects.' What use is that when the rejects result from poor tools, maladjusted machines and inferior materials? If those factors were remedied, the system would produce few defects.

Point 11: 'Eliminate numerical controls for the workforce'

Workforce here means all staff. As regards production workers, Deming argues that work study targets are a nonsense. Such targets are based upon the average worker, yet statistically, half of the work force will perform above average and half below average. Peer pressure will restrict above-average performers from producing to their full potential, while below-average workers will struggle to meet their obligations.

Work study calculations ignore quality. Bank clerks, says Deming, work to standard times for everything, and everyone is rated daily. Time matters more than caring about the task and relating to customers. Likewise, Deming is emphatically opposed to piece-work, which he argues is an incentive to produce scrap and thereby destroys pride of workmanship. Creating pride of workmanship, says Deming, is the most difficult part of improving quality.

Deming argues that the only permissible numerical targets are those based on fact, such as 'Unless sales can be increased by 10 per cent, we shall be out of business next year', and, 'The law now requires us to limit carbon dioxide emissions to 1 per cent.' Even here, it is pointless for top management to set a target and then leave everyone else to get on with it.

The system must be changed to ensure targets can be met.

For example, anyone can show a reduction in stock holdings, simply by paying the supplier or some other agent to hold goods. Genuine reductions, however, require a wholesale redesign of manufacturing systems, ordering procedures, and so forth.

Deming and performance appraisal

Deming is opposed to merit rating, because it:

- Rewards people for manipulating the system rather than improving it.
- Is often self-defeating.
- Is inconsistent with team-work.
- Acts as a substitute for proper management.
- Is inherently unfair.

Merit rating forces employees to concentrate upon achieving short-term results, a practice which is seldom consistent with quality. For example, investment fund managers are judged upon quarterly index performance. This highly public assessment tempts them to find ways of 'nudging' figures upwards to give the impression of out-performing other fund managers. In the long run, however, the client suffers, as constant switching of funds entails high risk for the sake of fractional and transient gains. Far better to buy shares with long-term potential and wait, ignoring daily price fluctuations.[11] Such is the system, however, that fund managers cannot afford to advise clients in their true best interests. Likewise, rating police officers upon numbers of convictions tempts them to seek easy pickings and to ignore the more intractable cases. It may even lead to perjury. Crime prevention is the last thing such a system produces. Counts, argues Deming, are an easy substitute for meaningful measurement. Besides, fair rating is virtually impossible, as performance depends upon multifarious factors, most of which are beyond an individual's control.

Rating, Deming argues further, obstructs team-working because it breeds selfishness. In meeting its targets, Department A does not care about the problems caused to Departments B, C, and D. Pursuit of self-interest can destabilise the organisation.

Deming's alternatives to rating

- Meticulous selection of leaders.
- Educating leaders in their obligations, and improved training and education after selection.
- Getting leaders to function as colleagues rather than as judges.
- Subordinate performance to be assessed using statistical data.
- Annual three- to four-hour interviews with subordinates, aimed at support and encouragement.
- Accommodation of lone workers.

Most of these points are self-explanatory. Deming's philosophy is built upon Statistical Process Control (SPC). SPC is a technique whereby objective data are analysed statistically in order to determine system capability and functioning. Deming argues, for example, that raw employee output figures are meaningless. Someone who scores say 10 is not necessarily performing worse than someone scoring 15. What counts is whether performance is within statistical control or otherwise.

Point 12: 'Remove barriers that rob people of pride of workmanship'

Deming argues that annual performance and merit-rating are the biggest obstacles to pride of workmanship for salaried staff. Shop-floor workers are even worse off, because they are the victims of a whole range of managerial shortcomings. These are:

- Confusion over what constitutes acceptable workmanship.
- Pressure to meet quotas.
- Foremen and inspectors devoid of product knowledge.
- Instructions to 'run it' ie make a defective product.
- Cheap tools and poor machines.
- Delays, shortages of components and defective supplies.
- Management attitudes that, since staff are being paid, why should they care about the inadequacies of their supplies and equipment?

- Poor supervision, resulting in accidents and therefore unnecessary cost.
- Inadequate job knowledge.
- Bad drawings, out-of-date drawings, changes to instructions and rush jobs.
- Inadequate support from technicians and engineers.
- Unfair and/or nonsensical rating systems.

Deming argues that instilling pride in workmanship automatically prompts operatives to contribute to improving the system.

Point 13: Encourage education and self-improvement

Deming urges organisations to invest massively, not only in job-related training but also education in its broadest sense.

Education which is unrelated to an employee's job may be the most critical of all.

Although it is unclear why this should be so, Deming seems to be suggesting that narrowly defined criteria for return upon investment reflect short-term thinking, and that the real pay-off is in employee satisfaction:

> People require in their careers, more than money, ever-broadening opportunities to add something to society, materially and otherwise.[12]

Point 14: Take action to accomplish the transformation

Deming's fourteenth point concerns how to implement the preceding thirteen. Deming urges organisations to proudly adopt the new philosophy, and to communicate its implications to everyone in the organisation. Above all, *patience is essential.*

Deming emphasises that change takes time. Organisations must recognise that improvements can take five years or more to accomplish.

Although every organisational activity is part of the system and must therefore receive attention, Deming suggests that *organisations should begin by concentrating upon activities with the biggest potential for improvement.*

The recommended approach is summarised in the Shewart cycle, shown in Figure 1.

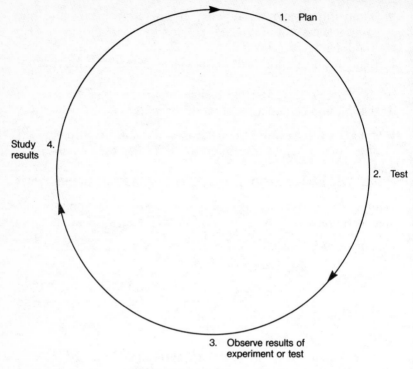

Figure 1 The Shewart cycle

The cycle begins by managers identifying potential accomplish-ments and what these entail. Stage two is experimental, tests are made, or the change is implemented on a small scale. The results are observed and then studied. What was learned? What can be predicted? Informed by this new knowledge and understanding, the cycle is repeated in perpetuity.

A SUMMARY OF DEMING'S FOURTEEN POINTS OF MANAGEMENT

1. Create constancy of purpose for improvement of product and service.

2. Adopt the new philosophy.

3. Cease dependence upon inspection to achieve quality.

4. End the practice of awarding business on the basis of price alone. Instead, minimise total cost by working with a single supplier.

5. Improve constantly and forever every process for planning, production and service.

6. Institute training on the job.

7. Adopt and institute leadership.

8. Drive out fear.

9. Break down barriers between staff areas.

10. Eliminate slogans, exhortations, and targets for the workforce.

11. Eliminate numerical quotas for the workforce and numerical goals for management.

12. Remove barriers that rob people of pride of workmanship. Eliminate the annual rating or merit system.

13. Institute a vigorous programme of education and self-improvement for everyone.

14. Put everybody in the company to work to accomplish the transformation.

3
DESIGNING FOR QUALITY

Quality is a virtue of design.[1]

Customer satisfaction results from:

- quality of design;
- quality of conformance to design.

Conformance has received considerably more attention in the literature than the quality of design itself. This is surprising, because design is the more important of the two. This is because:

- design determines the product features which give satisfaction or dissatisfaction;
- conformance is easier to achieve with a good design than with a bad one.

The rationale for these two points will emerge as the chapter proceeds. Here, it is sufficient to say that no amount of care during production and delivery can compensate for a poor design. Many design faults are irremediable. Some models of car designed for left-hand drive, for example, are difficult to adapt to right-hand drive. One of the consequences of such ill-conceived designs is that the clutch cables on right-hand drive models are prone to breaking because of their tortuous routing through the engine compartment.

Achieving an attractive good design on paper is one thing; translating it into reality is another. The notorious Hulme housing estate in Manchester, for example, received prizes for its architecture. No doubt the terraces and walkways looked most impressive on the architect's boards, yet the design contained a number of fundamental flaws. Failed wall joins, for example, led to damp penetration which meant the flats were continuously cold and clammy despite huge heating bills. The unpatrolled 'walkways in

the sky' proved eminently suitable for muggers and criminals flee-
ing arrest and eminently unsuitable for refuse collection and other
essential services. Although hindsight is the only exact science
known to man, the probability of achieving a good design can be
substantially enhanced by applying the concepts and techniques
outlined in this chapter.

QUALITY AND LOSS: THE STARTING POINT OF GOOD DESIGN

Quality design begins with minimising loss. Taguchi defines quality
as the loss imparted to society once a product is delivered.[2]

The aim of a good design is to minimise loss once the customer takes delivery of the product.

A shirt, for instance, imparts a loss every time it must be washed
and ironed. The longer it takes to iron, the greater the loss; the
more power an electrical appliance consumes, the greater the loss.
A car which has a service interval of only 6,000 miles imparts a
greater loss than one which will run for 20,000 miles without
requiring attention. A drill which takes five minutes to assemble
results in greater loss than one which takes only two minutes to
assemble. A television which incurs ten seconds 'blipping time'
results in potential loss as follows: (10 seconds) × (say 4 times per
day) × (365 days) × (8 years of life expectancy) = a loss of 32
hours. Although such figures are small in themselves, in aggregate
they can represent enormous wastage. Moreover, the customer
may not be the only person to suffer. Certain losses, such as
exhaust emissions, vehicle noise, the effects of nicotine and so
forth are incurred by the whole of society.

The thief in the night

Taguchi argues that certain forms of loss are nothing short of scan-
dalous. Manufacturers sometimes try and maintain price levels by
surreptitiously reducing the product specification, ie the mid-
point of the tolerance level, by a small amount. Taguchi argues
that this is worse than theft because:

When a thief steals 10,000 yen the victim loses 10,000 yen so
there is neither gain nor loss to the whole society. But when

the mid-value is moved, the manufacturer imparts a larger loss, say a 20,000 yen loss – to consumers in order to make a 10,000 yen profit.[3]

To take an extreme example, reducing the thickness of the armour plating on a battleship by 0.01 millimetres may save the manufacturer £250,000 per vessel but what is that set against the lives of the crew and the ship if the reduction in the specification increases vulnerability to enemy missiles?

Sources of loss

According to Taguchi, loss emanates from either *functional variation*, such as a train that fails in snow, or *harmful effects* such as, the side effects of a drug. Sources of loss include:

1. **Power consumption** – the washing machine which is £50 cheaper to buy but uses 10 per cent more electricity imparts a greater loss in the long run than the apparently more expensive model.

2. **Life expectancy** – the pair of fashion boots which last for only one winter impart a greater loss than more robust footwear.

3. **Maintenance, reliability and 'trouble'.** A council-owned housing estate where the landscape design incorporates shrubs and bushes imparts a greater financial loss than plain grassed areas, not only because of maintenance requirements but because shrubs and bushes act as litter traps which must be cleared periodically. When something breaks down there is not only the cost of repairs, but the cost of being without it. In some cases the latter can be many times more than the purchase price of the machinery. Moreover, the cause of a breakdown may be trivial. A whole broken-down engine is worth no more than the 2 pence part that happens to have failed.

4. **Space requirements or occupation with volume** – personal computers impart a greater loss than notebook computers because they cost more to house and their relative bulk restricts their use.

5. **Positioning or set-up time** – the time required, for example, to position a tin opener, to programme a video recorder, or to log on to a computer, counts as a loss.

Another way of conceptualising loss is to calculate the total cost of a product. Figure 2, for example, shows how this applies to car purchase.

The real cost of a product is not just the purchase price, but everything associated with it. In the case of a car this includes insurance, fuel consumption, depreciation, and so on. This shows how quality is a means to an end: *designing to reduce loss benefits both producer and customer*. The benefits are twofold. First, reducing loss makes a product more attractive, and therefore more competitive. Second, according to Taguchi, both parties experience a direct financial gain. For example:

- Cleaning cost £20,000
- Reduce to £10,000
- Add £1,000 extra cost and £1,000 profit.

The manufacturer is thus £1,000 better off and the customer £9,000 better off.

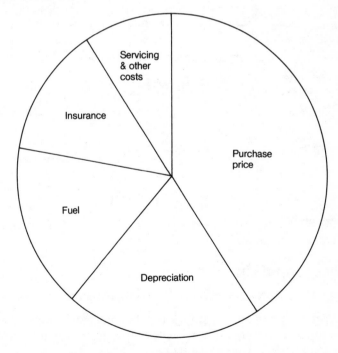

Figure 2 The total cost of buying a car

ATTRIBUTES OF A GOOD DESIGN

According to Taguchi, a good design reflects an optimal trade-off between cost and performance. A good design is one which is:

- cheap;
- operates well over a large range;
- is compatible with related products.

Cheap and simple

It is easy to make a design more complicated, but it takes genius to simplify a design.[4] The virtues of simplicity are many. Simple designs are cheaper to produce than complex designs, because complexity requires precision, and high precision is more difficult to achieve than low precision. Simplicity means minimising the number of parts in a product. Schonberger notes that the number of parts in new generation dishwashers, cars and watches have been reduced by up to two-thirds compared to old designs.[5] Construction, too, has been simplified. For example, instead of assembling parts with screws and fasteners, these can now be grouped into sub-assemblies and mounted upon moulded frames that snap together.

Costs are reduced as a result of:

1. Fewer suppliers, less administration and supplier supervision, and fewer supplier-related problems.

2. Quicker assembly and production.

3. Increased robustness.

4. Reduced costs as a result of 1, 2 and 3 and the benefits of standardisation.

5. Greater customer satisfaction as a result of 1, 2, 3 and 4.

Robust simplicity

Robust products are easier to manufacture.

Fewer parts, grouped into sub-assemblies, make products easier to manufacture and enhance their ability to tolerate variations in the production process.

Robust products give better service.

A product which functions satisfactorily over a wide range of conditions is more useful than one which performs exceptionally well only in one set of conditions.

Integration and process capability

Good design requires not only a clear customer focus, but must integrate with the organisation's technology, culture, market orientation, and so forth. Product design should be an opportunity for the organisation to lead from strength. This means that designers must take into account the *process capability* of their organisation. Process capability basically means: *Can we do it?*[6]

One of the earliest examples of process capability analysis was the compilation of the English 'Domesday Book' which assessed the tax-paying capability of each town and village. Other examples of process capability analysis include the study of form in horse-racing, election opinion polls, and credit referencing.

The time to discover whether capability exists is at the design stage. This is so obvious, and yet it is surprising just how many products and services are launched without the basic capability to pursue them.[7] Prudential's hasty entry into estate agency is one such example. Prudential knew nothing about the business. After buying-out numerous small private agencies at premium prices they then destroyed such capability as did exist by replacing local staff with new and inexperienced employees, ignorant of local markets. Within three years or so, Prudential sold many agencies back to their former owners for nominal sums, having made huge losses.

Process capability analysis must cover all aspects of an organisation's activities. It is not only an organisation's ability to produce a particular design which matters, but also whether it can distribute and market it. Where new products or services are envisaged, the organisation's skill and knowledge base are critical factors; such capability has to be cultivated like a garden. Money alone is insufficient, as the large investment houses discovered when they entered the financial services markets following deregulation in 1986:

A new trading . . . 'product' would be identified – Japanese equity warrants for instance. Next, a team of traders would be poached from another house. Then an off-the-shelf software package was installed to enable them to track their exposures. Banks' trading operations were built out of collections of these software 'modules' none of which were linked into any of the others. Finally, existing settlement staff were asked to provide back-up support, often for products they did not understand.[8]

Investment houses tried to beat the competition by continuously poaching the 'best' people and investing in computers, never acknowledging that no one really understood the new business. Instead of developing capability through training and on-the-job experience, many investment houses spent five years spending money to create incompetence.

It is critically important that managers ensure that the necessary process capability exists or can be developed in time. Hard evidence is essential. A simple but powerful approach is to differentiate between the following three categories of information:

1. Known.

2. Unclear.

3. Assumed.

There is, for example, a difference between obtaining confirmation that the bank will lend money to finance a project and *assuming* that it will oblige in this way. Assumptions are often unavoidable in decisions about process capability, but they become dangerous when people treat them as 'knowns'. Exposing assumptions is one of the most valuable roles a manager can play in capability analysis as people so easily forget that their 'knowledge' is but an assumption. We 'know' that the bus will take us to London because it says 'London' on the destination board. Yet we cannot be *certain* that it will do so again, however reasonable the assumption.[9]

ACHIEVING A ROBUST DESIGN

Taguchi emphasises that the variations a product experiences in manufacture are negligible compared with the variations it is subjected to once it passes to the customer. Whereas the concept of zero defects is based upon the idea that reduced variation in the manufacturing processes leads to reduced variation or failure in the field, Taguchi says:

Designing in order to reduce product failure in the field simultaneously reduces the likelihood of defects in the manufacturing process.

The logic of Taguchi's argument is as follows. The zero defects approach focuses managerial attention upon ensuring that processes are within acceptable deviations from targets, for example, plus or minus 0.001 millimetre thickness. Taguchi argues that any departure from the nominal value means a loss. A bar of chocolate which is slightly below the target value stated on the wrapper results in a loss to the purchaser. The manufacturer too may suffer a loss. For instance, the cumulative effect of so many underweight bars may mean boxes cannot be packed as tightly as they should be, resulting in damage in transit. Loss is also incurred if the bars are slightly above the mid-value. For instance, a surplus of three grams multiplied by 100,000 bars is 300 kilos of raw material, plus additional handling costs. The customer too may suffer a loss. Taguchi, for instance, quotes the case of the person on a diet eating a product which is three grams heavier than anticipated. Likewise, if some of the components of a car are above the mid-value the increased weight may result in greater fuel costs.

The real weakness of the zero defects approach, however, is that in any batch of products, a significant number will be close to the outer limits of the tolerance levels. Further, many of the other components which comprise the finished product will be in a similar state. This can play havoc with quality. Product engineers at Sony television, for example, discovered that viewers preferred a colour density of ten. Tolerance limits were therefore set at a minimum of seven and a maximum of thirteen. The televisions were manufactured at two locations. Those manufactured at location A were produced within the tolerance limits, whereas sets manufactured at location B were produced as near as possible to the target density of ten. Many of the televisions produced at location A proved to be barely acceptable because they had been manufactured at or near to the minimum of seven or maximum of thirteen nominal density. These sets required considerable maintenance throughout their lives and consequently resulted in a much greater loss than televisions produced at location B, which required only a few minor adjustments to render them satisfactory.

The consequences of variation in a system are potentially cata-strophic. A jet aircraft manufactured within the tolerance limits might contain a large proportion of components which are virtually defective. The result is known as a 'tolerance stack-up', ie where an otherwise harmless variation in one component exacerbates a varia-tion in another component, and so on. Catastrophe results where the total variation resulting from so many near-defective compo-nents interacting with one another reaches a point where the entire system breaks down.[10]

Consistency reduces the probability of catastrophic 'stack-up' because components all vary in the same way, even if they are all off-target. Conversely a product which conforms to plus or minus specifications is less robust, because the deviations are random and therefore unpredictable. For example, if a consignment of mushy peas is slightly undersalted, the fault can easily be rectified. Indeed, the customer is unlikely to reject the product, he will sim-ply add a little salt to compensate. If, however, in addition the quality of a proportion of the peas is marginal, the resultant 'tole-rance stack-up' may not only mean that the product is unacceptable, but that the damage is irreversible.

DESIGN DECISIONS: SIGNAL TO NOISE

Televisions emit both a signal and a noise. The signal consists of the sound and picture; it is the desired part of the transmission. The noise is the unwanted part of the transmission: for example, susceptibility to interference from other appliances, and a 'shaky' screen. Taguchi applies the television analogy to designing for quality:

Quality of design may be measured as the ratio of signal to noise.

Signal is what the product or sub-component is intended to deliver. Noise is what impairs delivery. Sources of noise include the effects of interaction with other components or sub-assemblies, and environmental conditions. *Robustness is defined as a product with a high signal-to-noise ratio.*

Designers, argues Taguchi, should aim for robustness under extreme conditions because *products which perform well in adverse conditions usually prove hard-wearing in normal use.*

Approaching design

In order to optimise signal-to-noise ratios, Taguchi advises:

- Identify the product's objective. Choose or develop the most apposite signal and calculate the corresponding noise.
- Identify as many options as possible for the critical design characteristics, eg size, power-to-weight ratio.
- Choose the option providing the most robust design or the highest signal-to-noise ratio.

SPEEDING UP THE DESIGN PROCESS

The pressure

Product obsolescence is a major problem for many organisations. The enormous pressure to innovate and market new products quickly means that the danger of ill-considered designs passing into production is high. The problem is exacerbated by a phenomenon known as escalation.[11] As Figure 3 shows, costs increase exponentially once a product passes from the design phase into testing and production. The whole organisation becomes involved, finance is raised, advertising campaigns are planned, equipment is purchased, advance orders are taken, and so on. The process is extremely difficult to reverse and the longer it continues the greater the probability of bad designs becoming bad products. The problem for organisations, therefore, is how to innovate quickly but soundly.

Making haste slowly

Exhorting designers to work faster or to cut corners is counterproductive. Although a 'ramped up' organisational culture may help, the real solution is to recognise that *whilst some parts of the design process can be speeded up, other parts need to be given more time*.

Concept design is the most important phase and the one which is least amenable to pressure, as it requires originality and fresh thinking. Designers bled dry are no use to anyone. They should be encouraged to feed their intellect and imagination by undertaking travel, study visits and so forth, without the expectation of an immediate payback. Further, they need to work in an atmosphere

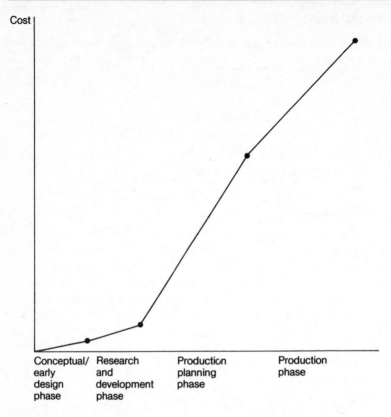

Figure 3 The escalation of costs during design and production

where mistakes are regarded as progressive and where painstaking, high-quality work is valued.

The research and development phase focuses upon new materials and new processes required to translate the design concept and ambitions into a workable model. Product design involves translating the model into detailed specifications and drawings. These latter phases of the design process can be speeded up by:[12]

■ Integration.
■ Removing sources of delay.
■ Concurrent planning.

Each of these is now discussed in turn.

Integration

Integration involves the creation of interdisciplinary teams encompassing design, manufacturing and marketing staffs. Hitherto, for example, engineers at Ford Europe would develop the basic product. Once this was complete, designers then added the so-called 'wrap round'. Then the manufacturing section had to work out how to produce it. Incorporating the three functions in one department and carrying them out simultaneously has reduced the lead time for new products by over one year.[13] Casio too have integrated their operations, in order to enable them to cope with rapid obsolescence.[14]

Removing sources of delay

Over-control is a major source of delay, so:

- Keep the brief clear and simple.
- Minimise the amount of detail in design specifications.
- Ensure designers understand customer needs and production capabilities.

The purpose of a design brief should be to liberate designers. It should therefore be confined to essentials, ie specifying a maximum of three or four variables. The team responsible for designing the Honda City Box Car, for example, was simply told to produce a small, energy-efficient car that would sell well.[15]

Concurrent planning

Quality requires attention to all aspects of a product. Design must therefore consider a wide range of issues, including:

- Customer performance specifications.
- Design specifications.
- Manufacturing specifications.
- Sales specifications.

These, too, should concentrate on essentials, those *features which are important to the customer*.

As Ishikawa notes, a ball-point pen has 600 characteristics.[16] It would take years to specify each of these precisely, and by the time the task was complete the product would be obsolete. Again, the list of essential features will seldom contain more than three variables. Further, concentrating on essentials prevents energy from being dissipated on details with a corresponding effect upon customer satisfaction. As Deming notes, few motorists care whether their car door conforms to 0.0001 mm tolerances or 0.01 mm tolerances; what matters is that the door closes with a satisfying thud, the seals are waterproof, the engine is sufficiently powerful, etc.[17]

Beware specifying even essentials too tightly. Fine tolerances, Deming argues, are rarely necessary, and only make the problem of controlling variability needlessly difficult.

Aim for 'loose tolerances tightly enforced', rather than 'tight tolerances loosely enforced'.[18]

If a customer insists upon tight tolerances, ask why he needs them.[19] Rigid specifications are often a power ploy by which to 'screw down' the supplier. In practice, the power is unusable because customers never have time to check that a product conforms to the 300 criteria listed. The best approach is to persuade the customer that it is in his interests to allow the manufacturer more flexibility. Better quality and reduced costs are powerful arguments. A most effective means of expressing them is to point out to the customer how much those tight tolerances are costing him.

THE HARE OR THE TORTOISE?

The hare

Some industries depend upon radical innovation for survival. Others may need to choose between a highly innovatory strategy, or one based upon continuously upgrading existing products or services. Dramatic change is exciting and can confer the following advantages:[20]

- A decisive lead in market share.
- It introduces 'new blood'.
- There is little dependence on employee involvement, as few are able to contribute meaningful ideas where new products or other major innovations are concerned – indeed, such involvement might only hinder progress.

There are drawbacks, however. The saying about never being first with any new invention is well-founded. Prestige comes at a price. The price includes:

- Major investment.
- High risk.
- Major discontinuity.

Innovation typically requires massive investment in research and development, with no guarantee of return. Add to this the opportunity cost of committing the entire organisation to the project. Innovation and quality are not synonymous. New inventions may not prove as popular as anticipated, or perform as well as anticipated. The massive readjustment required to develop new products or services means only minor improvements to quality are subsequently feasible, because organisational energy is absorbed in re-establishing equilibrium. Meanwhile competitors exploit the inventor's success by developing improved versions of the original without incurring the risks and expense of research and development. It has been suggested that America's poor competitive record is explained by the fact that they *can* put a man on the moon. Although the Americans invented the transistor and the colour television, their world market share of sales of these goods is now less than 50 per cent, and falling.[21]

The tortoise

An alternative strategy is to concentrate upon making small improvements everywhere, including methods, product reliability, marketing techniques, speed of delivery and so forth. Interestingly, although radical innovation is incompatible with continuous improvement, *an incremental strategy does not preclude drastic change*. Indeed, it has been suggested that it actually improves organisations' capability to innovate radically.[22]

EDUCATING CUSTOMERS

The best design in the world is useless if the customer is insufficiently knowledgeable to gain the benefit of it, or if it is inappropriate to his needs. Customer education is therefore an important part of sales design and is usually under-emphasised. Education means more than pointing out the special features of a product such as the lights under the car seats. Education involves:

- Ascertaining why a customer wants a particular product.
- Supplying technical data with sales literature.
- Drawing the customer's attention to such data.
- Explaining in clear and simple language the significance of technical data.
- Drawing attention to and explaining improvements to design.
- Training staff to initiate technical discussions and respond to technical enquiries.

A product which is excellent for one purpose may be useless or even dangerous for a different but related use. Never assume that a customer is aware of the differences between products. All sales discussions should begin by clarifying a customer's needs. Some hand-held computers, for example, are excellent for storing vast quantities of information but have poor note-taking facilities, while other models possess the reverse characteristics. The former are useful for entering data, such as inspections results or cash till transactions, but almost unusable for longer compositions such as notes and memoranda. Since both types are described as 'hand-held computers', customers can easily make the wrong choice. Likewise, not all freezers incorporate a 'fast-freeze' facility. This is no problem for someone who only wants to store frozen food, but a customer who wants to freeze food needs a 'fast-freeze' function.

Good products are often undersold because their real worth is unappreciated.

Real worth exists not in advertising slogans but in performance specifications and other technical data. Yet technical data are difficult to obtain, especially where consumer goods are concerned. Moreover the customer almost invariably has to ask or even press for such information and, unless the customer is familiar with technical terms, even when he obtains the information, its significance may well be lost upon him. Rarely are sales staff able to help. For instance, when I was shopping for a compact disc player, enquiries about channel separation, compatibility with existing system and so forth produced only blank stares, embarrassed 'Don't knows' and useless 'Should be OK's' from shop assistants. Such ommissions mean that products supported by heavy advertising tend to capture the market, while better and cheaper designs can languish for want of customer knowledge.

It is extremely short-sighted intentionally or unintentionally to sell a product which is inappropriate for a customer's needs. To do so is to destroy trust and confidence, and with it any prospect of repeat business and recommendations. Aim instead for the customer who says:

> A friend said 'Go to So and So' when I needed a word processor. They asked me what type of work I would be using it for and then explained what I would need and fixed me up with a powerful enough PC, a good printer, and good software. I would recommend them to anybody.

This advice is especially relevant to retailers. Although manufacturers selling by mail order are trying to develop customer relations capability, the major advantage retailers possess is their ability to discuss a customer's needs with him, supply the right product and help the customer through the initial teething troubles which are inevitable with complex products such as computer equipment.

COMPLETING THE CYCLE: LEARNING FROM THE CUSTOMER

The designer's most important teacher is the customer.

However much though and care go into the design of a product, what matters is how it performs in service. Small-scale testing is useful, especially in the early stages of evolution, but only the combination of the finished design and direct exposure to actual conditions provides a truly reliable test. Extensive pre-production testing is therefore vital. Most of the design work upon British Rail's Advanced Passenger Train, for example, was tested on a short test track. It was only when trials were conducted in service conditions that designers realised they had made a fundamental error. The train's tilting system resulted in passengers complaining of nausea. Since the design was based on the tilting system, the project was abandoned.[23]

A customer's perceptions of quality are influenced not only by the product *per se*, but by a whole range of factors including installation, maintenance and usage. Designers therefore need to know how a product is treated once it leaves the factory. In-service testing and feedback are further sources of information for the ongoing design process.

Seeing how a customer uses a product can stimulate innovation. A manufacturer of high quality leather goods, for example, discovered that one of their products, a leather portfolio case, was often adapted by customers for a variety of purposes. This information prompted designers to create a new range of products based upon customers' varying adaptations. Observing customer behaviour can save designers much time and effort. Architects, for example, have long realised that the best way to design footpaths is to observe the routes people take to get from one place to another and then to construct paths accordingly.

The quality of after-sales support is an important feature of design. Such support might include teaching the customer to use the product, providing an effective help service, training repair staff, ensuring replacement parts are readily available at a reasonable cost, and good product warranties. A good way to start is to imagine yourself alone on a Sunday afternoon with your product. You cannot get it to work and yet you need it, desperately. What sort of care and attention would you welcome?

Finally, the hundreds of people who bought the product are important but what of the thousands who went elsewhere? The tourists who frequent a boarding house year after year matter, for example, but what about those who go next door?

The most important customer is the one who did not buy.[24]

It is dangerous to rely solely upon repeat business. Customers go out of business, grow old, get divorced, emigrate, their tastes and incomes change, and so on. Over time, one by one, they fall away. A recent survey of small solicitors' firms, for example, found that practices which concentrated upon providing a given level of service to a specific circle of clients were dying for want of replenishment, exacerbated by competition from other firms.[25] Likewise, manufacturers of high-performance sports cars are currently discovering that brand loyalty and snob appeal are insufficient to retain customers in the face of strong price competition from the Japanese. The reasons for rejection may be hurtful, but it is the unwelcome experiences which most often stimulate learning and growth.

A stable clientele is a shrinking clientele.

SUMMARY

■ Design is the foundation of quality because:

— it determines the product features which give satisfaction or dissatisfaction; and
— good designs are easier to manufacture than bad ones.

■ Quality design aims at minimising loss from a product once it leaves the factory.
■ Reducing specifications to increase profits results in a disproportionately high loss to the customer.
■ Loss emanates from either functional variation or harmful effects.
■ Sources of loss include:

— power consumption;
— life expectancy;
— maintenance and reliability;
— space requirements;
— set-up and positioning times.

■ Designing to reduce loss benefits both producer and customer.
■ A good design is one which is:

— simple;
— cheap;
— operates well over a large range;
  and
— is compatible with related products.

■ It is important to ascertain that process capability exists or can be developed before embarking on a new design.
■ Designing for product reliability in the field simultaneously reduces the likelihood of defects in the manufacturing process.
■ Consistency reduces the probability of catastrophic 'stack-up'.
■ Quality of design may be measured as the ratio of signal to noise.
■ A robust product is one with a high signal-to-noise ratio.
■ Products which perform well in adverse conditions usually prove hard-wearing in normal use.
■ The early phases of the design process require most time.
■ Later phases of the design process can be speeded up by:

- — integration;
- — removing sources of delay, notably control;
- — concurrent planning.

- Radical innovation is exciting, but it is highly risky and inconsistent with continuous improvement.
- Continuous improvement does not preclude radical change – it may even facilitate it.
- Manufacturers sometimes unwittingly undersell their products, through failing to educate customers.
- Customer education should include:

  - — ascertaining why a customer wants a particular product;
  - — supplying technical data with sales literature;
  - — drawing the customer's attention to such data;
  - — providing clear and simple explanations of the significance of technical data;
  - — drawing attention to and explaining improvements to design;
  - — training staff to initiate technical discussions and respond to technical enquiries.

- The designer's most important teacher is the customer.
- The most important customer is the one who did not buy.

4

CONFORMANCE TO DESIGN

The previous chapter focused upon designing quality into a product. This chapter discusses the factors involved in ensuring that the product consistently meets the design specifications. Quality management may be defined as 'A systematic way of guaranteeing that organised activities happen in the way they are planned.'[1] The emphasis is on planning, for 'Good things only happen when planned; bad things happen on their own.'[2]

Quality is a product of the system, and therefore the system must be designed to guarantee that requirements will be met. If the system is unsound, defects and even catastrophe are inevitable. The Clapham Junction railway disaster, for example, was caused by a signal giving an erroneous 'all clear'. The immediate cause of the disaster was the failure of a technician to repair a wire properly. The inquiry, however, revealed a series of underlying system failures which led to the accident. These were:

- The technician had been allowed to work seven days a week for many months.
- Workloads were not properly planned, hence the excess overtime and pressure to complete jobs.
- No one inspected the work and no one was responsible for inspection.
- Standards for insulation and testing were inadequate.
- Communications were inadequate, ie circulation of written instructions instead of proper training and communication.

Interestingly, despite these inadequacies, British Rail claimed to have implemented TQM.[3] Clearly, things are not always what they seem.

Conformity means consistency

Living as we do in an age of mass production, most people take consistency for granted. We assume, for example, that every fork in a canteen of cutlery is identical. Likewise we expect that beans from one tin will taste exactly the same as beans from another tin of the same brand. On a different level, we rely upon the pharmacist to administer our prescription correctly. Likewise, when passing traffic-lights we depend for our lives upon consistency between green and red signals, although we seldom think about it.

Achieving consistency, day in day out, is no mean feat – hence the phenomenon, for example, of 'Monday morning' and 'Friday afternoon cars'. The problem for manufacturers is that consistency depends upon being able to control and co-ordinate tens and sometimes hundreds of variables, all of which may interact with one another in an infinite variety of combinations.

Figure 4 depicts the three elements of a production system.

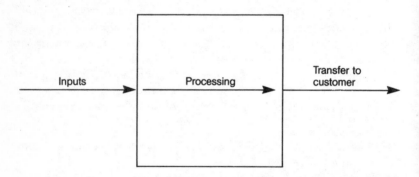

Figure 4 The three elements of a production system

The system basically involves the transformation of inputs into a product which must then be transferred to the customer. Production systems are rather like sausage machines, ie *you only get out what you put in; but unless you are careful, you may not even get that.*

Inputs, ie the quality and quantity of the pork, rusk, and so on are the first determinant of quality. The process can enhance quality; for example, the way in which the ingredients are chopped may contribute to taste and flavour. Likewise, rapid transportation may be used to maximise the customer's enjoyment.

Pause now and imagine the opposite, ie all the things that can go wrong in producing a batch of sausages. Good ingredients, for example, are worthless if the machine fails to mix them adequately or the product is tarnished through contact with metal or debris from a previous mixing. Even if the sausages are produced to perfection, they can easily be damaged before they reach the customer, by incorrect storage, inappropriate wrappings, and so forth.

Now reverse the thought process and imagine how you might ensure that every batch conformed to requirements. You might, for instance, want to set out all the ingredients in the correct quantities and in the correct order. You might instruct the operative to thoroughly inspect the machine before using it, and so on. Such planning is the essence of a quality management system. It can be applied to virtually any activity, from assembling circuit boards to organising a house removal.

Planning reduces the need for precision in control.[4]

Returning to the sausage machine analogy, if the ingredients are set out, the instructions are clear, the equipment is adequate and so on, then reliance upon supervision and inspection is reduced.

Figure 5 depicts the difference between conventional ratios of planning to control and those favoured by leading Japanese manufacturers.

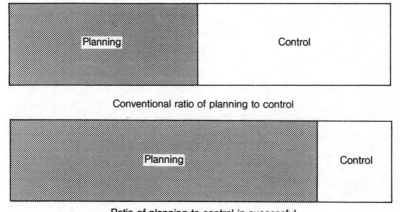

Conventional ratio of planning to control

Ratio of planning to control in successful
Japanese companies

Figure 5 'Old' and 'new' ratios of planning to control

Whereas traditional manufacturers rely heavily upon control techniques such as inspection and the threat of sanctions, the emphasis in leading Japanese companies is upon designing foolproof systems. Planning not only benefits quality and reduces the direct cost of defects, but savings accrue from employing fewer inspectors and supervisors.

Planning concerns more than the actual production process. It must focus upon matters such as conveyance of materials and parts, installation procedures, diagnostic routines, adjustment techniques, inspection methods, intervention criteria and methods, programme modification rules and preventive maintenance policies. For example, if a component is found to be close to being defective, then a procedure must exist whereby intervention occurs before the system starts producing defects. The precise nature of the intervention must also be determined. Adjustment may enable the process to be restarted, but unless the problem is correctly diagnosed and remedied, the loss continues.[5]

The point is, consistency can never be the product of a happy accident. The owner if a holiday cottage, for example, must ensure that every time new guests arrive storage cupboards are clean and empty, fresh towels are available, carpets are vacuumed, soap powder and other supplies are topped up, and so on. Hitting the target every time means:

■ ensuring supplies are available;
■ providing staff with a comprehensive check-list;
■ ensuring staff understand what stipulated standards mean in practice.

No one can work without tools. There is more to good management, however, than merely providing the necessary equipment. Provision must be organised to optimise productivity and minimise the risk of error. For instance, supplies can be organised in order of use.

Providing a check-list enables staff to both work efficiently and to check their own work. For instance, the check-list may instruct the employee to empty all bins first and then dust throughout, if it is quicker to proceed this way rather than room-by-room. Ticking off tasks as they are completed draws to the attention of the employee any omissions. Even the simplest of standards is open to interpretation, and therefore part of the planning process is ensuring the employee knows exactly what is required. What, for example, should a clean bathroom or cooker look like?

Without such planning, written procedures degenerate into meaningless bureaucracy. Check-lists and the like are useful in helping staff to adhere to standards, but it is futile relying upon pieces of paper to control quality. For example, when the customer takes delivery of a car he may sit with the salesman as they complete the check-list. 'Is the car in a satisfactory condition throughout?' The 'yes' box is ticked, despite the fact that the wrong number plates have been fitted! The weakness in the system which resulted in the mistake being made in the first place is never exposed, as the salesman cashes in a favour with the garage and the number plate is discreetly changed. The paperwork is handed in duly completed and, unless the customer complains, and he may well not because he is reluctant to get the salesman into trouble, everyone is duly satisfied.

Even if the 'No' box was ticked, it would probably make little difference, for who checks the check-lists? How often are customers delayed in taking delivery of a product whilst the sales clerk completes a long form muttering, 'Dunno why we have to fill these in, no one ever looks at them'?

Short-cuts to quality planning are in any case self-defeating. Managerial energy is absorbed in imposing unnecessary control, instead of taking a lead role in making improvements. A whole administrative infrastructure may be needed to move paper from one part of the organisation to another – a non-value-adding exercise. Employees are alienated, and are concerned first and foremost with observing the ritual of form-filling, instead of focusing attention on the customer.

THE ROLE OF DOCUMENTATION

The quality manual

It is advisable to document requirements. Quality planning is usually encapsulated in a quality manual. Briefly, the quality manual should consist of the following sections:[6]

1. Overall quality manual.

2. Departmental quality manuals.

3. Specific written procedures for all operations.

4. Purchasing specifications.

5. Lists of approved suppliers.

6. Product or service specifications, including subsidiary components.

Getting started

Quality planning begins with a statement of the organisation's quality policy. This expresses the general philosophy of the organisation and will seldom occupy more than a page – ideally substantially less. For example:

Quality Policy

R & W Health Care aims to achieve the highest standards of health care in the world.

This aim shall be achieved by commitment to research and staff development.

Although this is the shortest part of the manual, it is arguably the most important, because:

■ it sets the atmosphere for quality planning;
■ it is the page which readers, including customers, see first.

Indeed, the quality policy may be a customer's only evidence of the organisation's commitment to quality (apart from the excellence of the product or service, of course), as it is usually impractical to publicise the whole document.

The next section of the quality manual defines responsibilities for standards, control of documentation, procedures for systems review and amendments to the manual. It is basically intended to link the organisation chart to quality planning. This section might, for example, identify the person responsible for various types of decisions and contain details of the interdepartmental quality committees.

The third section of the manual contains specific work instructions for all operations. Work instructions are an important component of quality planning, as they define standards. For example:

All goods which arrive at Gowertronics Ltd are received at goods inwards. The goods will be placed on the appropriate shelf in the goods inwards area to await inspection.[7]

Items in stores are kept on shelves marked with the appropriate labels. These identification labels should be transferred to the cartons or boxes in which the items are packed.[8]

It is important to be systematic in setting out instructions. A sound approach is to structure the explanation as follows:[9]

1. What the task involves.

2. Why it is necessary.

3. When it should be executed.

4. Who is responsible for execution.

5. How the task shall be performed.

COMPILING QUALITY MANUALS

Preparing a quality manual does not by itself lead to improvements in quality.

Quality manuals are dangerous if they merely reflect an ideal. This is because they enable the organisation to delude itself into believing it has a system which guarantees improvement, when nothing has changed or ever will change. For example:

Manpower resources and facilities in the company are periodically and systematically reviewed against past, present, planned and forecast levels of business activity by product type, volume and mix to determine and regulate the forward programmes of recruitment and training from which manpower resources will be met.[10]

This looks good on paper, but what is the reality behind the rhetoric? As a former head of personnel, for instance, I found that periodic and systematic reviews against present levels of business activity meant discovering on Friday night that all the bricklayers had left to go and work on more lucrative contracts in the south of England. (This was in the boom times.)

Obviously there is nothing wrong with setting out the ideal;

quite the opposite, as it forces managers and employees to com-municate vision. It is only useful, however, if systems are designed whereby the ideas can and will be implemented.

In compiling work instructions, it is necessary to strike a balance between under-specifying and over-specifying.

A manual which is vague will fall into disuse because it is unhelpful. The same will happen with a manual which is too detailed, because it will be too big for easy reference; the more words used, the greater the potential for contradictions and confu-sion, and the greater the likelihood of instructions soon becoming hopelessly out of date. For example, take the directive on p 67 concerning goods inward. Which is the 'appropriate' shelf – the one nearest the door, where the rain blows in – or the one in the corner, where the roof leaks? Further, when does the operative put the goods on the shelf? Does he do it immediately, regardless of the fact that he has a customer on the telephone, or does he attend to the customer first, knowing that meanwhile the goods are in the way of fork-lift trucks and are vulnerable to damage?

The solution to this problem lies not in the design of the quality manual, but in training. The employee should know how to prioritise work and should possess sufficient technical and opera-tional knowledge to exercise sound judgement and initiative. The purpose of the manual is to structure training, to serve as an *aide-mémoire*, and to provide a basis for monitoring adherence to standards.

The more specific the manual the more effective a work-to-rule.

The history of industrial relations is rich in examples of how employees can turn an organisation's own power against it by rigid adherence to rules. Clearly the best answer is for the organisation to maintain good employee relations, to avoid the possibility of a 'work-to-rule'. However, it is nevertheless prudent to imagine the possible effects of industrial action. For instance, if the instruction states 'Adhere label using Perkins Patent Paste', in a work-to-rule there would be no question of substituting tape or glue, or even a different brand of paste, if the specified one was unavailable.

The best quality manual is one that is out of date.

Continuous improvement implies continuous change, which

means that the quality manual is forever out of date. This poses a problem for organisations, because the quality manual possesses a quasi-legal status, in that nothing may be varied without express authority. In practice this may involve considerable bureaucracy. For example, in some organisations ideas must be approved by a series of committees before procedures can be changed. This can be a daunting prospect for employees, and may tempt them to suppress their initiative, as it is too much trouble to pursue a suggestion.

One possible compromise is to relate the level of formality to the implications of the idea. A proposal which has organisation-wide implications requires approval at all levels, whereas a suggestion which only affects the immediate workplace can be authorised at that level.

ANTICIPATING ERROR: THE POKA-YOKE SYSTEM

Obtaining conformity to standards is traditionally regarded as one of the functions of an organisation's compliance system. While enforcement of discipline has a part to play, *designing for conformance should be concerned more with anticipating human error, than relying upon the threat of punishment to prevent it.*

Railway engineers, for example, have long sought to minimise the possibility of driver error, through the use of safety systems. For instance, a bell or a horn sounds in the cab whenever a train passes a signal, according to whether the signal reads, 'all clear', 'caution', etc. Unless the driver acknowledges the warning promptly, the train's brakes are automatically activated. The assumption is that the driver is motivated to operate the train safely; the purpose of the device is to help him to do a good job.

The Poka-Yoke system is based upon the same concept of 'mistake proofing'.[11] The aim is to engineer production to eliminate the possibility of error. Components for assembly can be designed, for instance, so that only the correct positioning will fit. Similarly, if ten items are to be assembled to form a product, the production system is designed to pass ten items to the operative. If the operative then finds one item left over, he knows that he has made a mistake and can correct it before any damage occurs.

The application of such error-prevention systems is by no

means confined to manufacturing. Pharmacists, for example, have long utilised a form of Poka-Yoke in drug interaction charts. Likewise it is becoming increasingly common for doctors to utilise computer data bases to check drug dosages, the correct treatment for a particular illness, and so on. Not only do such systems help prevent error by reducing reliance upon memory, they can lead to improved quality by enabling, in this case, the doctor to concentrate upon listening to the patient.

The four recommended principles for implementing Poka-Yoke are:

1. **Control at source** – Intervention should occur as near as possible to the source of potential defects, and always before a defective item is passed to the next stage of the manufacturing process.

2. **Maintaining a sense of proportion** – The more serious the potential defect, the tighter the system of control required. Where minor defects are anticipated, a warning light or alarm may suffice. Where potentially serious defects are anticipated, automatic shutdown of a machine or sub-operation may be justified.

3. **Simplicity and effectiveness** – Expensive automated inspection systems are seldom necessary or even useful. Improved production methods combined with simple controls are a more progressive approach.

4. **Do the obvious first** – Big problems are often the most amenable to simple solutions. Concentrate upon obtaining the greatest improvement for the least cost and effort. Shingo notes that, while design improvements can reduce defects in the long term, many Poka-Yoke devices can be installed within days, or even hours, thus providing an extremely useful and inexpensive stop-gap until a more robust product can be developed.

THE ROLE OF INSPECTION

Inspection can increase defects

Although quality cannot be inspected into products, this does not mean that inspection has no role to play in production. It is a poor cook who puts a dish on the table without tasting it first. That said, inspection should never be used as a disciplinary mechanism. For example, a managerial clamp-down on defects will indeed produce a reduction in the number of rejects. However, this is only because operatives will refuse to process any component which is the tiniest bit suspect – even though it meets standards. Consequently, the ostensible decrease in defects at the final stage of production masks massive waste at the intermediate stages. Alternatively, such a clamp-down may tempt operatives to pass borderline and even defective products, in order to keep the figures looking good.[12]

The role of inspection

A good precept to observe when designing inspection systems is that *the customer is the ultimate inspector*. Generally speaking, then, the best form of inspection is one which reflects anxiousness to please. If you were hoping to impress an important visitor would you not be checking and double-checking here, there and everywhere? Effective control is dynamic control, fully alert, seeking and anticipating problems.

Moving from the spirit of an inspection policy to the letter, inspection serves three purposes. These are:

1. Problem identification.

2. Problem prevention.

3. Problem elimination.[13]

Effective problem identification requires checks at the completion of every stage of the production process. One possibility is for incoming components to be checked before being processed. Another is a system of self-checking by the person who made or processed a component.

A defect is like a headache, ie the symptom of a deeper malaise. The presence of a defective or borderline part should result in a thorough investigation to locate the cause of the problem.

A diagnostic tool

Since variability can arise from so many factors, it is important to be systematic in seeking to determine cause and effect. The so-called 'fish-bone' diagram shown in Figure 6 is an extremely useful diagnostic tool.[14]

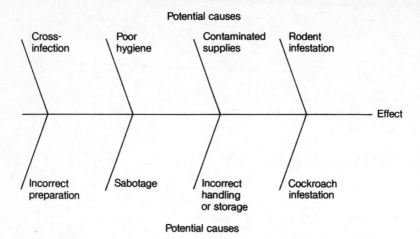

Figure 6 The use of a fish-bone diagram to identify the causes of an outbreak of food poisoning

Figure 6 is a simplified version of possible causes of an outbreak of food poisoning in a hospital kitchen. Identifying variables in this manner enables the investigator to begin by examining the most likely cause, and to work backwards until the diagnosis is complete. Bear in mind the following caveats:

- Are all possible causes listed?
- Is the problem as obvious as it seems?
- Could there be multiple causes?

If this sounds trite, re-examine the fish-bone diagram in the light of the following information:

> Environmental health officers collected a dead rat from the kitchen. Post mortem examination revealed that the rat was infected with the salmonella virus responsible for the outbreak.

One might reasonably deduce that the source of the infection was the rat; after all, a strong correlation exists between rats and disease. Correlations, however, merely indicate that a relationship exists between two factors. By no means do they prove that A causes B, or that B causes A. As Figure 7 shows, the association could be explained by an unidentified third factor.

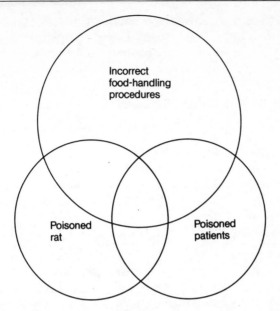

Figure 7 Unhygienic food-handling kills both patients and rat

As it turned out, the outbreak was caused by poor food-handling procedures, which had resulted in the food becoming contaminated. The rat had eaten some of the contaminated food and it too had been poisoned.

THE QUALITY MANAGER

Miracle worker

It could be argued that the appointment of a quality manager is contradictory to TQM philosophy, which stresses that quality is the responsibility of all employees and that the appointment of a quality manager merely allows other managers to abdicate responsibility for improvement. While this view is by no means unfounded, the stance taken here is that what matters is the level of the organisation's determination to change. If the employment of a quality manager is to be seen to be 'doing something', or is intended to effect a magical transformation, with only rhetorical support from senior management, then the appointment is bound to fail because the necessary commitment is non-existent. If, on the other hand, the organisation is genuinely seeking improvement, then a quality manager can play an extremely useful role, especially in the early stages of transformation.

The role of a quality manager

The post-holder can only be effective if suitably empowered, ie:

- Reports to the director or chief executive.
- Is a member of the management team.
- Shares responsibility for strategic management.
- Is briefed to involve himself in all aspects of quality in the organisation.
- Is properly supported by qualified staff and other resources.

The role of a quality manager is to enable other managers in the organisation to work towards improvements. In medium and large organisations the quality manager will probably be supported by a small team. The quality management function may be to:

- Encourage and facilitate quality improvement.
- Monitor and evaluate quality initiatives and progress towards attainment of improvements.
- Encourage the development of good relations with customers and suppliers.
- Plan, manage, audit and review quality systems and procedures.   .
- Co-ordinate or facilitate or provide training in all aspects of quality.
- Provide advice to managers and employees upon the establishment of quality systems and their control.
- Disseminate specialist and legal information pertaining to quality.
- Make recommendations for quality improvement.

The politics of quality

Regardless of what is said in the TQM literature about breaking down interdepartmental barriers, the appointment of a quality manager creates a potential source of tension. Quality managers are as hungry for power as every other manager. The quality manager seeks to build a power base by becoming the organisational witch-finder general, spying upon managers, seeking out and reporting upon examples of bad practice, identifying the recalcitrant, and so forth. Alternatively, the quality manager may try and establish control by insisting that all new proposals be directed through his office in order to 'assess the quality implications'. It is a small step from that to gaining control over all decision-making. Any attempt to curtail the quality manager's power will result in the accusation that the organisation is reneging on its commitment to quality.

Another potential danger is the development of a parent-and-child relationship between the quality manager and other managers. The parent complains that the child never tidies his room and doubts the child's fitness to assume independence. Yet the parent never sees that by tidying up after the child he is creating the very problem of which he complains. In such a situation everyone is dissatisfied. The quality manager feels both impeded and taken for granted. The line manager not only resents, as he sees it, the whole thing being taken out of his hands, but feels he could do a much better job than the quality manager if only he were allowed to.

In view of these potential difficulties, once quality consciousness is firmly established, it may be wise to dispense with a separate quality management function at the strategic level, and to decentralise the day-to-day quality management tasks. This enables the responsibility for quality to be shared, while ensuring that managers retain the necessary support in order to maintain manuals, comply with the law, organise training, and so forth.

SUMMARY

- Conformance means ensuring that requirements are constantly met.
- Planning is the key to achieving consistency.
- Achieving consistency requires control over all the factors which might affect a product's quality.
- The production system consists of inputs, the transformation process and transferral to the customer.
- Planning reduces the need for precision in control – aim for an 80/20 ratio.
- Planning must incorporate every aspect of a process.

- The aim of planning is to ensure employee efforts are all clearly focused and well directed.
- Check-lists should complement training, not substitute for it.
- Quality planning involves specifying requirements and procedures for all parts of production.
- It is advisable to document requirements.
- A quality manual normally contains:

  — the organisation's policy on quality;
  — details of responsibility for decisions;
  — specific work instructions.

- Quality manuals should reflect existing practice – not ideals.
- Documentation must strike a balance between being too vague and too detailed.
- The best quality manual is one that is out of date.
- Good systems are those which anticipate human error, instead of relying upon threats to prevent it.
- The four recommended principles for implementing Poka-Yoke or error prevention systems are:

  — control at source;
  — maintaining a sense of proportion;
  — simplicity and effectiveness;
  — concentration upon the obvious.

- Inspection can increase defects.
- Effective inspection is dynamic and ever-vigilant.
- The purposes of inspection are:

  — problem identification;
  — problem prevention;
  — problem elimination.

- The fish-bone diagram is a useful diagnostic tool.
- Cause and effect relations are seldom simple; problem diagnosis requires time, patience and an open mind.
- The appointment of a quality manager may help in the early stages of transition.
- Quality managers are only useful if properly empowered and if quality remains everyone's responsibility.
- The appointment of a quality manager may create counterproductive tensions.

5

QUALITY CERTIFICATION

QUALITY MANAGEMENT SYSTEMS

BS 5750 and ISO 9000 are becoming increasingly recognised as symbols of quality in both manufacturing and service industries. Certification is now virtually mandatory in some sectors, and it is a potentially decisive factor in winning contracts and custom. Since BS 5750 and ISO 9000 are identical, for simplicity the term BS 5750 is used throughout. It is stressed that the coverage, including that in the Appendix on page 80, is intended to supply general knowledge only. Organisations seeking to obtain certification and/or precise details should consult British Standards documentation.[1]

HISTORICAL BACKGROUND

Written quality standards date from the early part of the twentieth century and were first adopted by the defence industries in Great Britain and America. The initial aims were to provide products manufactured to clear specifications – to facilitate product interchangeability and to reduce production costs. Early standards therefore focused primarily upon product specifications rather than the production system.

The earliest quality management system dates from 1963. It is an American military standard, entitled *Military Specification, Quality Program Requirements*. This system became the foundation of all subsequent standards, including BS 5750.

BS 5750 was introduced in 1979. It was the product of various government initiatives dating from a 1967 White Paper entitled *Public Purchasing and Industrial Efficiency*. The White Paper was aimed at raising standards of quality assurance among government contractors. It recommended, for example, that purchase specifications should detail performance requirements. The document anticipates Deming's later work by suggesting that systems of quality control should replace inspection by the purchaser. A further major impetus was the 1977 Warner Report, entitled *Standards and Specifications in the Engineering Industries*. This report recommended the development of a national quality-management system, in order to eliminate the plethora of standards and assessment procedures.

PURPOSE OF BS 5750

BS 5750 basically aims to prevent 'non-conformity at all stages from design through to servicing.'[2] Subsidiary objectives include:

- To specify quality management system requirements.
- To provide a basis for contracts between purchaser and supplier.
- To enable any type of organisation to establish a clear, written, and practical quality management system.
- To provide a means of ascertaining the capability of a prospective supplier.
- To raise standards by promoting quality as a competitive weapon.

ACCREDITATION REQUIREMENTS

BS 5750 accreditation is via assessment by an approved certification body. The requirements for accreditation are contained in the BSI documentation which is available, at a charge, from the British Standards Institution. Briefly, BS 5750 consists of five parts. The most important is Part 4, 'Guide to BS 5750 Quality System' as it contains the requirements for accreditation.

Accreditation requires organisations to demonstrate capability to meet customer requirements.

Capability rests upon providing satisfactory evidence of:

- Clear systems, procedures and working methods.
- Clear systems of communication.

- Clear delineation of responsibility.
- Comprehensive documentation of all systems and procedures.
- Control of documentation and clear procedures for change.
- Adequate training in job-related skills and quality management.

All operations must be capable of meeting requirements. Assessment therefore includes subsidiary functions such as finance, marketing and personnel.

The BS 5750 quality-systems model consists of 20 elements. To give the reader a flavour of what BS 5750 certification entails, each element is explained briefly below. The full requirements are set out in the Appendix to this chapter.

1. **Management responsibility** – To define the organisation's quality policy in writing and to indicate how it is communicated throughout the organisation.

2. **Quality system** – To establish and maintain a documented quality system.

3. **Contract review** – To establish and maintain procedures for contract review and the co-ordination of associated activities.

4. **Design control** – To establish and maintain procedures for the control and verification of product design.

5. **Document control** – To establish and maintain procedures for control of all documentation and data pertaining to BS 5750 requirements. All documentation to be reviewed and approved by authorised employees prior to issue.

6. **Purchasing** – To ensure that all purchases conform to requirements.

7. **Purchaser-supplied product** – To establish and maintain procedures for verification, storage and maintenance of purchaser-supplied items for use in production.

8. **Product identification and traceability** – To establish and maintain procedures for product identification at all stages of production, delivery and installation.

9. **Process control** – To ensure that production and installation are planned, documented and carried out in controlled conditions in accordance with BS 5750.

10. **Inspection and testing** – To ensure no incoming product is used or processed prior to inspection or verification. Verification to be carried out in accordance with written procedures.

11. **Inspection measuring and test equipment** – To control, calibrate and maintain inspection, measuring and test equipment. Measurement uncertainty to be clear during use and in accordance with requisite measurement capability.

12. **Inspection and test status** – The status of a product to be clear at all times, to ensure that only products conforming to requirements are despatched, used or installed. Conformance or non-conformance to be indicated by appropriate markings, for example, tags, labels, routing cards and inspection records. Records to identify the individual responsible for product release.

13. **Control of non-conforming product** – To establish and maintain procedures to prevent accidental use or installation of non-conforming products.

14. **Corrective action** – To establish and maintain procedures for the investigation and rectification of all instances of non-conformity.

15. **Handling, storage, packaging and delivery** – To establish and maintain procedures for handling, storage, packaging and delivery of products aimed at preventing damage or deterioration.

16. **Quality records** – To establish and maintain procedures for record-keeping and usage to facilitate easy access and prevent loss, damage or deterioration.

17. **Internal quality audits** – To plan, execute and document a comprehensive programme of internal quality audits to ascertain whether quality activities conform to planned arrangements, and to evaluate the quality system's effectiveness. To ensure the results of audits are communicated as appropriate and acted upon promptly where necessary.

18. **Training** – To establish and maintain procedures for the identification of training needs. To ensure training needs are met and records maintained.

19. **Servicing** – To establish and maintain procedures for servicing and for ensuring that servicing meets requirements.

20. **Statistical techniques** – To initiate procedures for determining suitable statistical techniques to check process capability and conformance to product specifications.

WHERE TO START

The BS 5750 document is intended as a model for all types and sizes of organisation. The process of obtaining accreditation begins with translating the model into a framework suitable for the organisation. It is advisable to obtain specialist assistance with this task. Effective consultants will meet the following requirements:

- Possess detailed knowledge of BS 5750.
- Be experienced in interpreting BS 5750 requirements generally.
- Be experienced in implementing BS 5750 within similar organisations.
- Possess membership of the Institute of Quality Assurance.

Organisations may proceed as they wish. Successful applicants typically observe the following programme:

1. Education and training in quality in general and BS 5750 in particular.

2. A comprehensive review of all organisational systems and procedures.

3. Design and documentation of new systems and procedures.

4. Pilot-testing.

5. Review and modification as required.

6. Full-scale implementation.

7. Audit of procedures and activities.

8. Implementation of necessary corrective action and review.

Obtaining accreditation requires time and much painstaking work. Here is an example of the requisite level of detail:

Storage of Items
All items are received through the 'Goods Inward Inspection' function. It is the responsibility of the stores clerk to check that all items are identified to a job number by writing the

number on to the item itself using a marker pen or other material, provided it does not damage the item.

It is the responsibility of the stores clerk to ensure that identification marks are clearly legible and not likely to be adversely affected by normal stores operations. Stores items, whether in stores or stored elsewhere, are identified by the stores clerk in accordance with stores' records. All employees are responsible for ensuring that identification labels stay on items and for reporting deficiencies to the stores clerk or works manager. The stores clerk or works manager must remedy the deficiencies immediately.

Samples of all documentation must be included in the quality manual, including the format for internal audits, a specimen certificate of conformity and even such things as identification labels.

IS IT WORTH IT?

For many organisations the question is academic, as certification is a contractual condition. Given the growing number of organisations seeking accreditation, it is foreseeable that uncertificated ones will find it increasingly difficult to win business.

However, *BS 5750 is not a panacea for survival.* Useful though accreditation is, BS 5750 is more concerned with the establishment of systems than with their merits. For example, organisations are required to document working methods and to train employees accordingly. The efficacy of those methods is immaterial, provided they are capable of meeting customer requirements. Meeting requirements is insufficient in a competitive environment. The key to survival is improvement, delighting the customer, not merely satisfying some mechanistic criteria.

Obtaining accreditation is like passing a driving test. The emphasis is upon satisfying the examiner rather than learning to drive. Theoretically, obtaining accreditation is a dynamic process. In practice it is more likely to result in conservatism than change. This is because:

- It detracts from the more fundamental aspects of quality, such as product design.
- It tempts organisations to make the best of existing systems and procedures.

■ It tempts organisations to rest upon their laurels.

On the first point, BS 5750 leads organisations to ask questions such as 'How are we going to get our stores procedures certificated?', instead of asking how stocks might be eliminated. Such is the work involved in obtaining accreditation that organisations are unlikely to look beyond streamlining existing practices. Consequently, although the certified organisation is better than the pre-certificated one, the opportunity cost is the wholesale improvement which might have resulted from demolition and reconstruction. Obtaining accreditation can tempt organisations to conclude that they have 'done enough' about quality. Further, finding a receipt for certification discourages organisations from subsequently essaying drastic change because of the potential risks and difficulties involved in obtaining approval for new systems and procedures.

Certification therefore provides only a limited guarantee of quality. BS 5750 has its weaknesses, which some organisations exploit. For example, there is no requirement to appoint a quality manager *per se*, nor is there any requirement for the management representative to be of senior status or professionally qualified. Some organisations are more interested in the benefits of accreditation than commitment to quality. Once certified, their observance of procedures is minimal. Although the aim of engaging a BS 5750 accredited supplier is to eliminate the need for rigorous examination, it is nevertheless prudent to examine the reality behind the certification.

This is not to suggest that obtaining certification is a cosmetic exercise – far from it. The very act of identifying responsibilities, training needs, setting out work methods, developing documentary control and so forth necessarily result in a better-managed organisation. Success breeds success: *the real value of BS 5750 is as a means to an end.*

Seeking accreditation enables organisations to demonstrate their commitment to quality to employees and to involve them in change. The work of clarifying systems forces managers to acquire a deep understanding of processes and of the difficulties faced by employees. Improvement, involvement and understanding foster employee relations. Seeking accreditation can provide the foundations of a quality culture. As with all resources, *it is not what you have that counts, but how you use it.*

SUMMARY

- BS 5750 and IS 9000 are becoming increasingly recognised as symbols of quality.
- Early standards focused upon product specifications rather than the production system.
- The aims of BS 5750 are:

  - to specify quality management system requirements;
  - to provide a basis for contracts between purchaser and supplier;
  - to enable any type of organisation to establish a clear, written, and practical quality management system;
  - to provide a means of ascertaining the capability of a prospective supplier;
  - to raise standards by promoting quality as a competitive weapon.

- BS 5750 basically requires organisations to demonstrate that their systems are capable of meeting customer requirements.
- Evidence of capability includes:

  - clear systems, procedures and working methods;
  - clear systems of communication;
  - clear delineation of responsibility;
  - comprehensive documentation of all systems;
  - control of documentation and clear procedures for change;
  - adequate training.

- All organisational operations are assessed.
- The BS 5750 quality-systems model consists of 20 elements, ie:

  - management responsibility;
  - quality system;
  - contract review;
  - design control;
  - document control;
  - purchasing;
  - purchaser-supplied product;
  - product identification and traceability;

— process control;
— inspection and testing;
— inspection measuring and test equipment;
— inspection and test status;
— control of non-conforming product;
— corrective action;
— handling, storage, packaging and delivery;
— quality records;
— internal quality audits;
— training;
— servicing;
— statistical techniques.

Organisations are required, as relevant, to satisfy BS 5750 criteria pertaining to each of these elements.

■ Organisations may use any method they wish to obtain accreditation. The following model has proved effective:

— education and training in quality in general and BS 5750 in particular;
— a comprehensive review of all organisational systems and procedures;
— design and documentation of new systems and procedures;
— pilot-testing;
— review and modification as required;
— full-scale implementation;
— audit of procedures and activities.

■ It is advisable to obtain specialist advice before embarking on the process of obtaining accreditation.

■ BS 5750 is not a panacea for survival. There is an opportunity cost in obtaining accreditation.

■ When engaging suppliers, investigate the reality behind certification.

■ BS 5750 is best viewed as a means to an end, ie the foundation of a quality culture.

APPENDIX
THE REQUIREMENTS OF BS 5750/IS 9000

Element 1: Management responsibility

1.1 To describe the organisation's 'quality policy' in writing and to indicate how it is communicated throughout the organisation.

1.2 To describe the organisation structure indicating individual and sectional responsibilities and authority.

1.3 To explain how the organisation proposes to implement and monitor procedures for ensuring workmanship and products meet customer requirements.

1.4 To specify the role of employees within the organisation, and in particular, their:

— experience;
— qualifications;
— responsibility for quality.

1.5 To nominate a management representative to:

— act as a focal point for enquiries;
— to be responsible for the implementation of the quality system;
— ensure its continued effectiveness.

1.6 To explain how quality systems are reviewed and monitored at management team level.

1.7 To describe the recording methods pertaining to points 1.1 to 1.6.

Element 2: Quality system

2.1 To establish and maintain a documented quality system.

2.2 To identify the responsibilities of employees within the quality system.

2.3 To relate the organisation's operations to each of the individual elements of BS 5750: Part 1, 1987/ISO 9001/EN 29001.

2.4 To identify the responsibilities, commitment and participation of employees within the quality system.

2.5 To explain how the organisation's quality system is:

— implemented;
— updated;
— maintained.

2.6 To integrate the functions of management with the quality system.

2.7 To ensure that the quality system describes the organisation's approach to quality management.

2.8 To ensure the products of the quality system are consistent with customers' requirements.

Element 3: Contract review

3.1 To review all orders to ensure that customer requirements are clearly defined and understood.

3.2 To describe the organisation and documentation of contract review meetings.

3.3 To involve essential personnel and departments in decisions concerning the acceptance or rejection of customer orders.

3.4 To ensure that the process capability exists to meet contractual requirements.

3.5 To devise a system whereby changes to requirements can be properly co-ordinated, enacted and formally approved.

3.6 To explain how records are collected and maintained.

3.7 To identify responsibilities for the various aspects of contract review.

3.8 To specify criteria for ensuring the organisation is capable of processing a customer's order prior to its acceptance.

3.9 To explain the system for receipt and processing of orders.

Element 4: Design control

4.1 To identify a plan for design indicating:

— the tasks involved;
— responsibility for each task;
— checking procedures;
— time-scales for completion.

4.2 To ensure all plans are controlled, updated and approved by authorised personnel.

4.3 To ensure that all employees participating in design and development activities are appropriately qualified.

4.4 To commit sufficient managerial resources to design and development.

4.5 To establish the appropriate interfaces within design and development to ensure information is transmitted accurately.

4.6 To explain the procedure for receipt and initial processing of original design input documentation.

4.7 To ensure that all stages of the design and development process are properly documented and that adequate procedures exist for doing so.

4.8 To ensure that design and development requirements are clearly understood.

4.9 To ensure that authorised employees liaise with the customer in order to confirm that requirements are clear and sufficiently comprehensive, and that modifications are discussed and documented.

4.10 To specify the organisation's design procedures, including design review meetings, drawings, purchasing specifications and alternative calculations.

4.11 To specify acceptance and rejection criteria.

4.12 To ensure documentation is readily available to employees at all stages of design and development.

4.13 To implement a documented system for controlling design changes, including employees responsible for authorising such changes.

Element 5: Document control

5.1 To identify responsibilities for compilation, approval, issue, monitoring, recording and control of documentation and data pertaining to the quality system.

5.2 To devise a draft system for the compilation, approval and circulation of organisational procedures.

5.3 To establish a master file of current documentation and assign responsibility for its maintenance.

5.4 To establish procedures for the removal of obsolete documentation.

5.5 To ensure that documentation is readily available as required.

5.6 To ensure employees are trained to understand organisational documentation and data.

5.7 To explain how support documentation is controlled.

5.8 To create a control system for changes to documentation. Where possible, the originator to be involved.

5.9 To assign a unique numbering system to all documents.

5.10 To obtain customer approval of relevant documentation if contractually required.

Element 6: Purchasing

6.1 To explain the procedures whereby the organisation ensures that all supplies conform to requirements.

6.2 To ensure the organisation's purchasing requirements are clearly communicated to the supplier.

6.3 To create a system for the selection of approved suppliers and subcontractors.

6.4 To plan and instigate supplier auditing.

6.5 To create and maintain a central filing system for all supplier and contractor records.

6.6 If appropriate, to implement a system whereby the organisation can check products and services at the supplier's premises.

6.7 To nominate responsibility for all tasks involved in purchasing.

Element 7: Customer-supplied product

7.1 To issue written instructions for the control of items supplied by customers.

7.2 To provide segregation facilities to prevent any possibility of confusion with other customer products or stores items.

7.3 To check the customer's supplied item against pertinent documentation and record receipt.

7.4 To provide adequate handling and storage facilities.

7.5 To record and report instances of non-conformance of supplied item to the customer before processing/utilisation.

7.6 To ensure that customer supplied items are periodically checked for suitability if stored for any length of time.

7.7 To identify responsibilities for control, recording and maintenance of all activities involving customer supplied product.

Element 8: Product identification and traceability

8.1 To be capable of identifying all products.

8.2 To ensure identification indicates whether or not a product has undergone a particular operation or process.

8.3 To set out internal traceability procedures pertaining to the isolation of suspect products.

8.4 To ensure customer traceability requirements are planned and documented.

8.5 To identify responsibilities for product identification and traceability and associated records.

Element 9: Process control

9.1 To document work instructions, explaining how products or services shall be produced, including:

— any special requirements;
— working practices;
— samples of workmanship;
— criteria for acceptance and rejection.

9.2 To implement a system for ensuring products and services conform to requirements at all stages of production.

9.3 To implement a procedure for the commissioning of manufacturing processes and associated equipment.

9.4 To establish a comprehensive training programme for all personnel associated with process control.

9.5 To maintain records of all work instructions and to identify those relevant to quality planning requirements.

9.6 To identify any special processes, ie those requiring supplementary information, training, work instructions or inspection.

Element 10: Inspection and training

10.1 To implement inspection and testing procedures at appropriate stages of production and despatch.

10.2 To implement a recording system which clearly indicates that a product has satisfied acceptance criteria before it passes to the next stage of production.

10.3 To operate an inspection system at the following stages as appropriate:

— goods received;
— in process control;
— final inspection;
— audit inspection;
— 'first off';
— initial sample.

10.4 To implement a procedure for control of incoming products released on an urgent basis.

10.5 To provide quarantine facilities for products awaiting inspection.

10.6 To ensure no product can be despatched prior to inspection and recording of results.

10.7 To train employees in the proper use of measuring and test equipment.

10.8 To document the requisite tests, together with any special requirements such as equipment to be used, setting, calibration, etc. Documentation to be compiled by qualified and authorised personnel.

10.9 To implement a procedure for the control and filing of certificates of conformity.

10.10 To identify responsibility for the acceptance of products against specifications.

Element 11: Inspection measuring and test equipment

11.1 To document the calibration systems used by the organisation.

11.2 To provide suitable equipment.

11.3 To detail the method of calibration for various equipment.

11.4 To incorporate selection of measuring equipment as part of quality planning.

11.5 To determine intervals between calibration for all equipment.

11.6 To ensure all items of equipment possess a unique identification number and calibration record.

11.7 To ensure that employees involved in calibration are trained and clearly authorised.

11.8 To ensure that equipment deemed unsuitable is formally removed and destroyed.

11.9 To detail the methods for repair of equipment.

11.10 To detail the procedure for the introduction of new equipment.

11.11 To ensure calibration equipment conforms to national standards.

11.12 To ensure external calibration organisations are suitably accredited.

11.13 To ensure that all users of equipment are properly trained in its usage, storage and calibration system.

11.14 To record and retain all calibration certificates and other information.

11.15 To guard equipment from interference.

11.16 To ensure environmental conditions are suitable for calibration.

11.17 To instigate reviews of calibration systems and procedures.

Element 12: Inspection and test status

12.1 To establish a procedure whereby the status of a product, ie conforming or non-conforming, is clearly evident at all times.

12.2 To ensure that the status of products is clear throughout the manufacturing process; for instance, whether or not inspected, whether awaiting inspection or segregated as non-conforming.

12.3 Authorised employees to maintain verification records enabling products to be released to the next stage.

12.4 To ensure the status of all products passing from one stage to another is ascertained as soon as practicable.

12.5 To ensure that regular status checks are carried out by authorised employees.

Element 13: Control of non-conforming products

13.1 To ensure that any non-conforming products or workmanship are clearly identified as such with appropriate documentation, and segregated.

13.2 To establish a documented system for the control of non-conforming items.

13.3 To identify procedures for the review, evaluation and remedy of instances of non-conformity.

13.4 To ensure that defective items are removed from the work area and disposed of regularly.

13.5 To define responsibilities and authority for the investigation and correction of non-conformity.

13.6 To establish methods of control over rework/rectification and concession systems.

13.7 To implement a communication system whereby departments receive information about instances of non-conformity and related investigations and remedial action.

13.8 If contractually required, to ensure that the customer's approval is obtained for all non-conforming items referred for repair or concession.

13.9 To ensure all employees involved in the identification of non-conforming products receive adequate training.

Element 14: Corrective action

14.1 To document a procedure for the prompt investigation of the causes of defects and corrective action.

14.2 To provide written evidence showing how all instances of non-conformity are investigated and corrected in accordance with recognised problem-solving techniques. Where appropriate, to implement documentation to prevent a recurrence.

14.3 To identify responsibility for instigating remedial action.

14.3 To describe the system for recording customer feedback, service reports and remedial action.

14.4 To ensure that remedial action is appropriately documented.

Element 15: Handling, storage, packaging and delivery

15.1 To document a procedure for the movement of products and materials throughout the organisation.

15.2 To ensure that handling methods and transportation equipment are:

- adequately designed;
- safe;
- available;
- used.

15.3 To establish a location system for products in store, together with appropriate documentation for location, receipt and issue of products.

15.4 To rotate stocks and to review stores regularly to prevent product deterioration and damage.

15.5 To ensure packaging methods and materials are suitable.

15.6 To transport products to customers' premises in accordance with approved methods.

15.7 To prevent damage and deterioration during handling, storage, packaging and delivery. Where damage or deterioration occur:

- to reject and segregate the product(s) concerned;
- to investigate the cause;
- to implement remedial action in accordance with the appropriate organisational procedure.

15.8 To ensure that all employees responsible for handling, storage, packaging and delivery are adequately trained.

Element 16: Quality records

16.1 To document a procedure for the collection and storage of quality records which enables easy access.

16.2 To specify which records are to be maintained and for how long.

16.3 To make quality records available, internally and externally as appropriate.

16.4 To ensure all records are legible and suitable for analysis of product conformance.

16.5 To identify responsibilities for the storage, maintenance and indexing of records.

16.6 To make available, as applicable, subcontractor quality records.

16.7 To ensure that the storage facilities for records are adequate and suitable for the purpose.

Element 17: Internal quality audits

17.1 To establish regular internal system audits by qualified personnel.

17.2 To ensure that audits are properly planned and that communication takes place with the departments concerned.

17.3 To identify a comprehensive audit strategy whereby all elements of the system are reviewed annually.

17.4 To devise standardised documentation for planning and reporting audits and to issue reports to the appropriate personnel.

17.5 To ensure that remedial action is implemented promptly and evaluated.

Element 18: Training

18.1 To establish a documented procedure for identification of the training needs, to enable employees to perform in accordance with system requirements.

18.2 To ensure employees receive training in quality awareness and are aware of BS 5750 and the organisation's quality system.

18.3 To identify responsibilities for:

— the identification of training needs;
— the development of training programmes;
— subsequent recording and certification.

Element 19: Servicing

19.1 To produce service contracts, as required, in accordance with customer requirements and the organisation's recommendations.

19.2 To identify qualified and authorised personnel to compile service schedules which stipulate precisely:

— the operations to be checked;
— the methods of checking, including equipment to be used;
— the information to be recorded.

19.3 To implement an independent audit system to confirm that servicing practice conforms to customer requirements and to ensure that servicing activities are implemented in accordance with time-scales and procedures.

19.4 To ensure that all employees involved in servicing products are adequately trained.

19.5 To analyse all service reports and communicate findings to the appropriate function within the organisation.

19.6 To implement an independent auditing system by qualified personnel to confirm that servicing practice conforms to customer requirements, and that servicing is implemented in accordance with procedures and time-scales.

19.7 To ensure adequate resources are available for servicing.

19.8 To identify responsibility for:

— accepting customer servicing requirements;
— completion of documentation;
— liaison with departments carrying out servicing work.

Element 20: Statistical techniques

20.1 To document procedures and techniques for product sampling techniques and process capability analyses.

20.2 To identify a system for carrying out capability analyses on new and existing processes.

Note:
The points set out above are an interpretation of BS 5750 and IS 9000 requirements. The reader is advised to consult original BS documentation for precise information.

6

QUALITY IN SERVICE ORGANISATIONS

Service organisations can be defined as those which deliver their products personally to the customer – for example, banks, hotels, hospitals, churches, estate agents, solicitors, and schools. Service organisations are an important and growing sector of the economy. Like manufacturers, however, they too are vulnerable to competition.

WHY SERVICE ORGANISATIONS ARE DIFFERENT

In manufacturing organisations the customer is remote, whereas in service organisations *producer and consumer meet face to face*.

The meeting point is where the product changes hands. It is known as the *interface*. In a bank, for example, the interface is the transfer of monies from the cashier to the customer. Service organisations are more complex than manufacturing organisations becuase they are faced with both the task of 'manufacturing' their particular product, and with managing the interface.[1]

The complexity of managing service organisations is typically compounded by the existence of multiple interfaces. In a hotel, for example, receptionists, porters, bar staff and so forth each represent a separate interface. Likewise, a doctor's surgery usually consists of at least two interfaces, ie receptionist and physician, though there may well be others such as nurses, health visitors and pharmacy staff.

The concept of interface

Figure 8 shows how service organisations may be conceptualised as consisting of two parts, namely the production interface and the delivery interface. The production interface is where the service is 'manufactured', and the delivery interface is where interaction with the customer takes place. So in a restaurant, for example, the

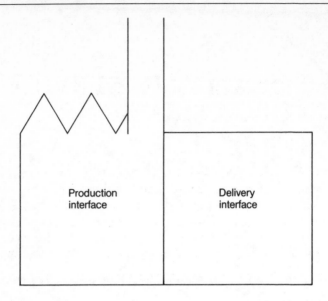

Figure 8 The two interfaces of a service organisation

kitchen is the production interface, which customers seldom see or enter. The reception, bar and dining room comprise the delivery interface where food and drinks are dispensed and where customers interact with representatives of the organisation. This chapter is primarily concerned with managing the delivery interface, as manu-facturing is covered in the rest of the book.

Organisations vary in the relative sizes of each interface. Strictly speaking, many manufacturing organisations are also service organisations, as producer and consumer do eventually meet. As Figure 9 shows, however, the delivery interface occupies only a small proportion of the total organisation of a factory, whereas in consultancy, for example, the proportions are reversed, as nearly all activities occur at the delivery interface.

Another method of conceptualising the two proportions of the organisation is to calculate *service intensity*, ie the cost of interface/ total cost, or alternatively, the amount of time spent with client/ total time. The higher the service intensity, the more critical the interface.

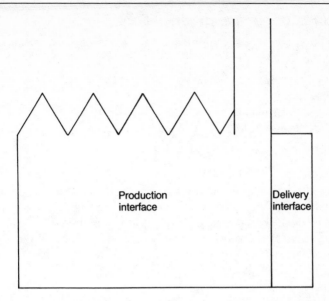

Figure 9a The proportions of production and delivery interface in a manufacturing organisation

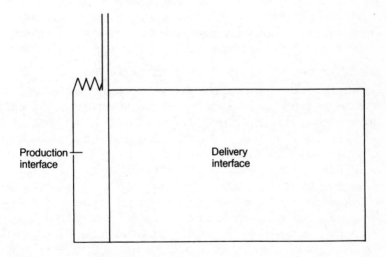

Figure 9b The proportions of production and delivery interface in a consultancy

Features of service organisations

Service organisations present special problems of management. These are:[2]

- Managing service delivery.
- Perishability.
- Interaction between producer and consumer.
- The intangible nature of quality.

Each of these is now discussed in turn.

Managing service delivery

Service quality is affected not just by the fitness of the product, but also by the manner of delivery. For example, a long sermon which loses the congregation's attention will be perceived as being of poor quality even though it may be theologically sound. Likewise, customers may desert a restuarant if the quality of service deteriorates even though the food is excellent.

Perishability

Planning services requires careful matching of capacity to demand, and this can be difficult to achieve. Unlike manufactured goods, services cannot be stored. If a patient fails to keep an appointment, the dentist's time is gone forever. Likewise, every empty seat on a flight or train journey represents an irrevocable loss of revenue. Conversely, insufficient capacity creates an equal or worse problem. Customers may go elsewhere rather than wait.

Interaction between producer and consumer

Customers seldom participate in manufacturing organisations, whereas in service organisations, interaction between producer and consumer is high. *Interaction affects perceptions of quality.*

Perceptions of quality in service organisations are believed to turn upon so-called 'moments of truth', when producer and consumer meet.[3] Such moments are critical because they can either be engineered to promote satisfaction, or, if mismanaged, can have the opposite effect. Restaurant menus for example, can be designed to stimulate discussion between customer and waiter and to create a favourable impression. If the waiter is rushed, however, or unable to answer questions, the customer is likely to be disenchanted, especially if he was relying upon the waiter's guidance.

Service organisations are expected to deliver a consistent standard, day in, day out. Many services must be performed 'on demand', even though conditions may be far from ideal. They are also relatively labour-intensive and therefore are vulnerable to the effects of interactions between employees, who are frequently required to work without immediate supervision. Service organisations must further contend with customers' moods and behaviour, and interactions between customers. Hospital out-patients, for example, may perceive staff as being uncaring because of their own heightened anxiety state. The behaviour of other customers may also create an adverse impression. Cinema-goers, for example, may be annoyed by chatter from other viewers.

Altogether, then, there is ample scope for things to go wrong. One of the interesting things about service organisations, however, is that *disaster can be turned into triumph*. Properly handled, a dissatisfied customer can become a devotee. Two hotel guests were once mildly disgruntled to discover their room had no towels. They reported it to a member of staff and were pleasantly surprised when, minutes later, the owner himself appeared offering profuse apologies. They were further cheered when they found that their next drink was on the house. They subsequently returned to the hotel year after year and told all their friends about it.

When things go wrong, the best advice is: *overcompensate*. Your reaction should be out of proportion to the complaint. As a child, I heard rumours that people whose bar of chocolate did not reach them in perfect condition received a whole box of chocolate bars in compensation. That is the sort of story which ought to be true. Such handsome gestures invariably pay for themselves in the goodwill they create, whereas the cost of a miserly response is incalculable.

Although long-standing customers can normally tolerate one or two bad experiences, the opposite is true of new customers. A mismanaged moment of truth with someone unfamiliar with the organisation can mean custom lost forever. How often does one hear people say, for instance, 'I went in there ten years ago when I was selling my first house. The receptionist was on the phone to his girlfriend. I stood around feeling stupid and then walked out. I never went back.' The best advice for managing new customers is to *spend a little extra time with them*.

Good hairdressers always devote an additional five minutes to speaking with a new customer, feeling the texture of their hair and testing how it brushes and combs. Likewise, a good vet meeting a pet for the first time will examine its general condition and talk to the owner about the animal's health and well-being. Quite apart from all the useful information gathered, people appreciate the attention, and a bond is created. The important point to remember is that first impressions are decisive.

The tone of a relationship is determined within three minutes of meeting.

Intangible nature of quality

Service quality is a highly subjective issue. What strikes one person as delightful informality is another's idea of rudeness. Similarly, one person may find the service in a restaurant relaxing whereas another may regard it as too slow. A customer's perceptions of quality may even rest upon factors which have little to do with either the product or the manner of its delivery.[4] This means there are critical elements of service quality over which the organisation can sometimes exert little or no control.

WHAT MATTERS MOST TO CUSTOMERS?

Although customer expectations are unique to the individual, they basically concern the *technical and functional aspects of the service*.[5]

The *technical* element concerns the manufacturing interface. The *functional* element concerns service delivery. The technical element of a hotel, for example, consists of meals, beds, lighting, mini-bars, carpeting, and so forth. The functional element pertains to the behaviour of managers, receptionists, waiters, rooming staff, porters and so forth. Research indicates that *the functional aspects of a service are the most important*.[6]

Staff behaviour has a critical impact upon perceptions of quality. This is not to suggest that the technical aspects of a service are unimportant, but the evidence is that hotel customers, for example, care a lot more about whether staff inspire confidence than whether the chairs are comfortable, or about the size of the bathroom towels. The hotel receptionist who dashes out to buy a newspaper for a customer who forgot to order the night before contributes more to customer satisfaction than comfortable seating and efficient tea and coffee arrangements.

The behaviours which affect perceptions of service quality are believed to be:[7]

- **Reliability** – Staff maintain standards day in day out, deliver promises and generally 'get things right first time.'
- **Responsiveness** – Timeliness, taking pleasure in providing service and showing a willingness to please.
- **Competence** – Staff possess the skills and knowledge necessary to perform the service.
- **Access** – Staff are easy to contact and are approachable.
- **Courtesy** – Staff exhibit consideration and respect towards the customer and his property; contact staff are neatly and cleanly attired.
- **Communication** – Educating and informing customers in plain language; listening to them.
- **Credibility** – Customer feels that staff are trustworthy and that they care about him.
- **Security** – Customer feels physically and psychologically safe.
- **Understanding** – Staff make efforts to understand a customer's needs and concerns; care is taken to provide for special needs or requirements; recognition of individuals, personalised attention.
- **Tangibles** – Facilities and equipment appear well-designed and maintained; personal appearance of staff; behaviour of other customers in the vicinity.

The first and last of the above points – reliability and tangibles – partly concern the functional elements of service delivery, but overall it is behaviour which counts the most. Research is still in its infancy, but it seems that of all the factors listed, *inspiring confidence is the most important*.

Instructors believe that driving tests depend less upon correct signalling, manoeuvring and so forth, and more upon whether the examiner feels safe when being driven by the learner. The same applies to service organisations. Clients need to feel confident that the doctor knows what he is doing; that telephone calls will be returned, that recommendations for work to be carried out are necessary, and so on.

Technical efficiency versus functional quality

Technical efficiency and functional quality can conflict with one another. The lone departmental typist, for example, represents high functional quality because users enjoy direct control, which is conducive to confidence. Technical efficiency, however, is low, in that the typist is sometimes under-employed and sometimes overloaded. The typist's accessibility results in frequent interruptions, as service users chase progress or ask him to do urgent jobs. Typing pools are theoretically technically efficient, in that centralisation creates economies of scale, enables workloads to be balanced and emergency jobs to be absorbed. Interruptions are avoided, as all contact is through the supervisor. Accuracy is higher, as staff can check one another's typing. The people who set up these organisations argue that the loss of functional quality is minimal, as turn round times and accuracy are guaranteed in service agreements.

Given those advantages, why do typing pools typically give a comparatively poorer service? Centralisation separates producers and consumers, whereas a departmental typist has direct contact with service users. Being immersed in departmental affairs, the typist understands the background to the work and is therefore more likely to recognise a mistake and less likely to make one. He knows what is urgent and how individuals like to see work set out. If he makes a mistake, he must deal with it, face to face with the person he has frustrated. The opposite applies to operatives in typing pools. When they type they see only words, and not the people or the issues and drama behind them. They know that if they make a mistake the document will come back, but provided they do not make too many mistakes, so what? In short *in service organisations, economies of scale are often an illusion.*

Large garages are typically much more expensive than small ones, and give an inferior service. The same goes for big chain hotels, chain car-hire services, nationally based estate agencies, and so on. The best practical advice when it comes to designing organisations for quality is to manage 'thinkingly':

- Apply conventional business school teaching critically, and be prepared to disregard it.
- In reviewing services, ask not what makes things easy, but what is making them hard?
- How much of the energy expended day in, day out actually adds value, and how much of it is just people making work for one another?

The reader may find it useful to consult chapter 7 for further ideas on improving efficiency.

MANAGING QUALITY IN SERVICE ORGANISATIONS

As with manufactured products, the key to quality in service delivery is customer satisfaction. In service delivery, *customer satisfaction means fulfilling expectations*. Fulfilling expectations means:

- Identifying important determinants of quality.
- Managing customer expectations.
- Managing impressions of product quality and service delivery.
- Customer education.
- Developing reliable support systems.
- Soliciting feedback.

Each of these points is now discussed in turn.

Identifying important determinants of quality

It is pointless to try and control the plethora of variables which affect perceptions of service quality. The best, and indeed the only thing to do is to *find out what matters, and concentrate upon providing it*.[8]

It is a mistake to try to be all things to all men. Some people base their wardrobes on designs which are neither too heavy for summer nor too light for winter, neither too smart nor too casual, and which match other clothes and accessories. A very sensible policy it is too, except that when they need to dress for an important occasion, they discover that they have nothing to wear! Some publicans make a similar type of mistake. By providing games rooms, children's rooms, function rooms, eating rooms for bar food, a restaurant for meals, there is something for everyone. The only thing that is missing is a special reason to go there. Contrast their folly with the wisdom of this former landlord:

> When I had a pub, there were no darts and no dominoes. No juke box, no singers and no pool tables. When you came to my pub, you came to drink. And I made a fortune.

Selection of a service organisation is usually based on one or two factors. Designing an appropriate service means asking:

- Who are our customers?
- What do they want?
- What can the organisation provide?

Airport catering organisations, for example, know that they have basically two types of customer: those who are in a hurry, and those with time to kill.[9] Refreshment facilities must therefore cater for the needs of both groups. Intercity rail travellers to London consist of those who need to arrive by nine-thirty am, and those who do not. Precise timings, and trains equipped with business and meal facilities, are more important to the former than cost, whereas to the latter group, the opposite applies.

Service provision must be consistent with organisational expertise and constraints of space, facilities, finance and technology. Aeroplane meals, for example, must be restricted to dishes which regenerate well in cook-chill systems and which can be well-presented given restricted space, plus heat and vibration. Disadvantages can be turned into marketing strengths. A locally based estate agency, for example, can compete with national chains by offering an owner-managed service. That one factor alone may yield a decisive edge.

Managing customer expectations

The story is told of an old barrister who had the same bottle of fine vintage port brought to his table every Christmas Day, invariably returning it to the pantry unopened. The rationale for this seemingly odd behaviour was that *no pleasure ever lives up to expectation*.[10]

The expectations which customers bring to an organisation have a critical effect upon their perceptions of quality. Someone arriving at a seaside boarding house is likely to be disappointed if he expects five-star hotel facilities. Conversely, someone expecting to receive half-board, ie breakfast and dinner only, and who then discovers the price includes morning coffee, is likely to be impressed.

Part of the role of management in organisations is to structure expectations. The best advice is: *undersell rather than oversell*.

Clients are often ill-served by estate agents' lyrical descriptions of their property. Although these may encourage prospective purchasers to view a house, reality is inevitably a disapointment and so people turn away when they might otherwise have bought.

Underselling does not mean going to the opposite extreme, but leaving a few pleasant surprises for the customer to discover.

Arousing expectations unrealistically can generate additional sales initially, but at the expense of repeat business and personal recommendations. The 'four-hour cleaner' and the 'on-time coach company' jeopardise their reputations every time they fall short of their self-imposed and often unnecessary standards. Tour operators likewise lose incalculable amounts of repeat business by painting idyllic visions of resorts, which are unrecognisable in reality. It is better to acquire a reputation for one or two factors which are important to customers, and to concentrate upon developing those.

Managing impressions of product quality and service delivery

Service delivery is like a theatrical performance.

The stage must be set and the staff must act the part.[11] Doctors can actually diagnose most illnesses just by asking questions. Much of the examination-couch poking and prodding is clinically unnecessary, but unless the ritual is observed, the patient feels worried. 'How does he know there's nothing to worry about? He never even examined me.'

Impression management explains why financial services organisations advertise that they will send someone 'mature' to discuss pension plans with prospective clients who are about to retire. Young staff command less credibility generally, and especially with older clients. Further, since youth is associated with ambition, they are more likely to be suspected of sales talk.

Educating customers

The importance of educating customers was mentioned in chapter 3. Similar comments apply to service organisations. Hotel guests in the West of Scotland, for example, occasionally reject their breakfast fish, saying it is 'off'. In fact, the problem is that the customers have never eaten really fresh fish. Continental lagers are generally more enjoyable drunk abroad, where they are served at the correct temperature, in the correct type of glass and poured properly. Clearly, *if customers are to gain maximum benefit from a product or a service, they must know how to use it.*

If hotel proprietors wrote a few explanatory notes on their menus, guests might boast about their breakfasts. Likewise, sales of continental lagers would probably rise if manufacturers educated customers. Besides, *to educate is to advertise.*

Education is a subtle and relatively inexpensive means of drawing attention to services. Solicitors, for example, distribute leaflets explaining the terrible consequences of dying intestate. Although the primary aim is educational, it does generate business. Education can also be used to create interest. The Toyota motor company has a place in Tokyo where people can see videos about cars, drive simulators, draw their own designs on a computer – anything except buy a car. Although the whole presentation is staged to promote Toyota, all suggestions of selling are deliberately suppressed. There are no salesmen or even any sales brochures. The strategy is to kindle excitement through allowing people to discover the product and the possibilities for themselves.

Developing reliable support systems

Technology should be designed to facilitate quality service. Staff cannot give the customer proper attention if their attention is distracted by equipment failures, or if they are impeded by antiquated or badly designed equipment. Yet how many shop assistants still add up on scraps of paper? The returns from improving systems can be substantially higher than intelligent guesswork might suggest. Customers' and management's ideas of acceptable waiting times may differ sharply. Reducing waiting times, therefore, can dramatically increase business.

Support systems should reflect customers' priorities.

It is important to discover which services can be automated without losing the personal touch and, most important, which ones cannot. Answerphones, for example, must be deployed with extreme care, as they seldom inspire confidence. Hotel mini-bars, on the other hand, are usually perceived as a benefit, as they enable guests to obtain refreshment at any time and to consume it in privacy.

Soliciting feedback

Measuring service quality is much more difficult than ascertaining the fitness of manufactured goods. Moreover, *the absence of complaints does not necessarily imply satisfaction.*

Although the same can be true of manufactured goods, these are more likely to be returned if they are unsatisfactory. Where service delivery is concerned, however, 'returns' are only a partial indicator of quality. Rather than make a fuss, many dissatisfied customers simply decide never to return. The organisation must therefore take the initiative and solicit feedback.

Research can lead you away from the truth. [12]

Inaccurate feedback is worse than no information at all. Here are just a few of the pitfalls:

- **Customers may not tell the truth** – How often have you been in a restaurant and been asked if everything is all right, and how often have you said 'Yes', while privately resolving never to return?
- **The wrong questions may be asked** – It is unrealistic to expect customers to complete detailed questionnaires. It is essential to limit the number of questions, but, in doing so, there is a risk of excluding important items. Moreover, questionnaire surveys are inherently limited in their ability to reflect respondents' feelings.
- **Replies may be biased** – Questionnaire completion rates seldom approach anywhere near 100 per cent. Since it is impossible to be certain of a truly random sample, the results may be seriously biased.
- **Problems of interpretation** – Having gathered the data, what do you do with it? The information is retrospective, and by the time it has been processed it may be too late to act upon. Besides, what is the data really saying? How does the knowledge that 250 of your 230,000 customers are satisfied with the service help?

This is not to suggest that organisations should not conduct research, but to emphasise the importance of ensuring efforts are well-directed. Well-directed research begins with asking: *what do I want to know?* [13]

It is sometimes said in research, better an approximate answer to the right question than a precise answer to the wrong question. The right question in this context is whether the customer is satisfied with those aspects of service delivery which are important to him.

THE IMPORTANCE OF FRONT-LINE STAFF

Front-line staff play a critical role in service delivery, because they:

- represent the organisation;
- are first to deal with crises;
- manage the potentially volatile customer interface.

The importance of front-line staff in service organisations is out of all proportion to their rank. As far as the customer is concerned, they often *are* the organisation. The Director of Operational Services rarely empties the dustbins. The Chief Constable seldom investigates household burglaries.

The key role which front-line staff play in organisations is seldom reflected in the quality of training which they receive. The reasons for this are discussed more fully in chapter 8. The root of the problem is preoccupation with short-term profits, which leads organisations to *concentrate upon artefacts rather than real quality*.

Service organisations often substitute control for training, stipulating, for example, the exact words to be used when answering the telephone. Standard responses envisage standard situations. Responding to critical incidents requires confidence and the ability to act independently. Many garages, for instance, employ front-line sales personnel who have no authority to negotiate. The idea is to minimise costs, employing untrained staff to do the 'soft' element of selling, such as demonstrating vehicles, while decisions on price are made by an unseen sales manager. Quite apart from the indignity this might cause front-line staff, this is hardly an effective way to conduct negotiations. Garages who operate such practices probably lose significant amounts of business as a result.

Many service organisations employ casual staff in order to minimise costs. Again, such parsimony is extremely short-sighted. The Western practice of treating casual staff casually merely creates a self-fulfilling prophecy.[14] Some estate agents, for example, now open on Sundays supposedly to offer a better service. Yet their weekend staff often receive no training or briefing, and therefore clients wishing to conduct negotiations or seeking anything other than basic information must wait until Monday when there is someone in the office who can respond.

A MODEL FOR TRAINING

Service organisations must recognise that *quality is a product of the system, and in service organisations, people are the system.*

How is a restaurant customer who asks for a cooler to preserve his expensive bottle of champagne impressed when the waiter replies, 'Isn't it cold enough?' The work carried out by front-line staff is much more complex than employers acknowledge. Playground assistants in schools, for example, are often better placed than teachers to detect bullying and other behavioural problems, but how often are they sent on training courses, or actively involved in the management process? Clerical staff in insurance brokers' offices regularly advise clients on claims, cover and liability, yet how many receive even the barest legal training?

To train staff is to create a formidable competitive weapon.

Doing so makes the difference between firing blind and hitting the target – every time. Imagine you rent a house, it is the middle of winter and the electricity has failed. The agent is out of town and the only person you can discuss the problem with is the receptionist. Which of the two is most likely to solve the problem, the receptionist who was employed straight from school and has learnt what she knows from working with other staff, or the receptionist who was employed straight from school but who has attended courses in assertiveness, problem-solving skills and communications skills? This is what the 'Right first time' rhetoric comes down to. Sustained excellence is not the product of chance or magic; it has to be developed in a systematic and well-directed fashion. The minimum requirements are:

- **Pre-experience training** – No one should be allowed to start work without basic skills training and briefing.
- **Skills training** – This should be based upon an analysis of the skills required to do the job *in practice*. The words 'in practice' are stressed, because job descriptions seldom reflect the real

work carried out by front-line staff. For example, 'Taking messages' may mean soothing anxious clients, presenting pointed communications in a diplomatic manner, communicating the intricacies of an issue to the recipient of the message, and so on. Training therefore has to be much broader than merely showing staff how to complete a message pro forma.

- **'On the job' guidance** – Time spent in training centres is only the beginning. Managers and training officers need to work with staff and train them as they do the job. This also helps remind the trainers of the difficulties which staff face.
- **Retraining** – Training must be ongoing. Skills do become rusty – as with driving, it is easy to slip into bad habits. Staff need to be kept up to date as standards improve and business plans change. Most importantly, continuous improvement means training staff not only for what they are doing, but for what they could be doing.

SUMMARY

- Service organisations are those which deliver their products directly to the customer, eg banks, hospitals, churches, insurance companies.
- Service organisations are an important and growing sector of the economy; they are vulnerable to competition.
- Unlike manufacturing operations, in service organisations producer and consumer meet face to face.
- The meeting point is where the product changes hands. It is known as the delivery *interface*.
- Most service organisations consist of several delivery interfaces.
- Service organisations present special problems of management. These are:
  - managing service delivery;
  - perishability;
  - interaction between producer and consumer;
  - the intangible nature of quality.
- Interaction between producer and consumer has a critical impact upon perceptions of quality.
- Service organisations are highly volatile but, properly handled, mistakes can be turned to advantage.

- Customer expectations can be divided into the technical and functional aspects of the service.
- The technical element concerns the manufacturing interface, the functional element concerns service delivery.
- The functional element is the most important.
- Quality is determined by:

  — reliability;
  — responsiveness;
  — competence;
  — access;
  — courtesy;
  — communication;
  — credibility;
  — security;
  — understanding;
  — tangibles;

  and, most of all, by inspiring confidence.
- Technical efficiency and functional quality may conflict with one another. However, the conflict is usually more apparent than real.
- The key to quality in service delivery is customer satisfaction.
- Customer satisfaction means fulfilling expectations.
- Fulfilling expectations means:

  — identifying important determinants of quality;
  — managing customer expectations;
  — managing impressions of product quality and service delivery;
  — customer education;
  — creating commitment to quality;
  — developing reliable support systems;
  — soliciting feedback.

- Front-line staff play a critical role in service delivery, because they:
  — represent the organisation;
  — are first to deal with crises;
  — manage the potentially volatile customer interface.

- Well-trained front-line staff are a formidable competitive weapon.

7

TIME

Man is nothing: he is at most, the carcase of time.[1]

Time is more than money, it is now a competitive weapon in its own right.[2]

Improving quality means improving production systems, which in turn exposes easier, better, and faster methods. The Japanese are now capitalising upon their lead in quality to minimise total production time. Total production time means the interval between placing an order and actually receiving the goods or service.

The Japanese have already made dramatic advances. A group of Western industrialists visiting a Japanese factory were asked how long they thought it would take to manufacture a washing machine. 'One week'. they said, doubtless wishing to flatter their host. 'Two-and-a-half hours', replied the production manager.[3]

Speed, like quality, is a means to an end.

The ends remain competitiveness and survival. Time is a powerful weapon, because it means more than customer satisfaction resulting from goods received sooner rather than later. Important though that is, the most significant benefits are:

■ reduced cost;
■ greater flexibility.

These two factors are interactive. The evidence is that quartering the time taken to produce goods and services doubles the yield of labour and working capital, which can mean cost reductions as high as 20 per cent.[4] Performance improvement requires wholesale reorganisation of production methods and logistics, including the reorganisation of manufacturing into small lots instead of conventional mass production. Small batch production facilitates flexibility, which means organisations can respond quickly and cheaply to changes in demand. This not only means they can offer the customer a wider choice of goods and services, but that waste emanating from over-production or holding stocks is reduced or even eliminated.

THE CONCEPTS OF TIME-BASED COMPETITION

Added value

Total production encompasses design, set-up, production and delivery. Speed of design is discussed in chapter 3. Here we are concerned with the other three elements of production. The key to time-based competition is not about driving people and machines faster, but about *the elimination of waste.*

Most people regard waste as materials ruined or discarded, and time which could obviously have been better spent. This view is partial: *waste is any operation which does not add value.*

Imagine all the parts of a car lying in a heap. Each part is worth so much – 5 pence, £3, £50 – whatever. The total value of individual parts is less than that of the finished vehicle, because batteries, gearboxes and so forth are of little use by themselves. As the car is assembled, however, each stage of the production process adds value. A painted car, for example, is worth more money than an unpainted one. The production process may therefore be viewed as a value delivery system.

Many Western value delivery systems are extremely inefficient. Figure 10 shows typical proportions of productive and unproductive time in manufacturing.

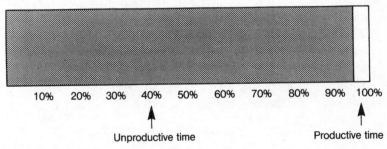

Figure 10 Typical proportions of productive and unproductive time in manufacturing

Only 5 per cent of the time spent working on a product adds value. In many organisations the percentage is even lower. A manufacturer of heavy lorries takes 50 days to prepare an order for assembly, but only 18 hours to actually assemble the vehicle. In other words, the product receives value for less than 1 per cent of its time in the system.

Sources of unproductive time

Sources of waste include:

- Tentative placement.
- Waiting time.
- Unnecessary movement.
- Over-production.
- Rejects.
- Set-up times.
- Transportation.
- Process waste.
- Materials waste.
- Communication.
- Administration.
- Untidiness.
- Bottlenecks.
- Bad timing.

Each of these is now explained in turn.

Tentative placement

Preparation adds only cost, never value. Figure 11 shows a typical allocation of time by activity when drilling a hole.

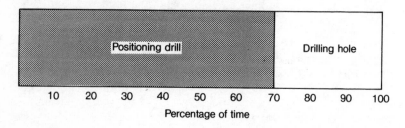

Figure 11 Loss of time through tentative placement

Seventy per cent of the time taken to drill a hole is spent loading and positioning the drill. The activity which adds value, ie boring through metal, accounts for only 30 per cent of the operation.

Obviously, improving some operations requires detailed and complex calculations. There are, for example, at least 27 different ways of drilling a hole in a table knife. That said, there are a great many operations which could easily be improved but continue to be done inefficiently because those responsible have no concept of the sheer waste, day in, day out. For example, imagine the difference between a stationery cupboard containing boxes of identical shapes and sizes, and one where shapes and sizes are mixed. Not only is the former easier and quicker to stock, it is also easier and quicker to use, and less likely to result in a time-consuming landslide.

A major reason for resistance to change is that inferior methods appear cheaper. Typewriters, for instance, are extremely wasteful, and yet numerous organisations still employ such antiquated technology, believing that a word processor is too expensive. Likewise, a small garage-owner I know has wasted half an hour every morning and every evening for the past ten years shuffling cars in and out of his workshop, which is too small and badly designed. He believes he cannot afford to pay the rent on proper facilities, although the Japanese experience is that improved work-design yields increases in productivity which far outweigh the costs involved.

Waiting time

There are two types of delay, the acute and the chronic. Acute delays are those caused by breakdowns in the system, such as shortages of materials, machine problems, and the secondary effects of the initial failure. Like an acute pain, the obvious disruption and costs stimulate intervention.[5] Chronic delay is defined as delay built into the system. It is the more invidious of the two, because it is many times more expensive and less obvious. Chronic delay escapes attention precisely because there is no disruption to alert managers. Ostensibly, everything is running smoothly; in reality there is massive waste. Figure 12, for example, charts the progress of a letter from a building society to a personnel department, requesting confirmation of an employee's earnings for mortgage assessment.

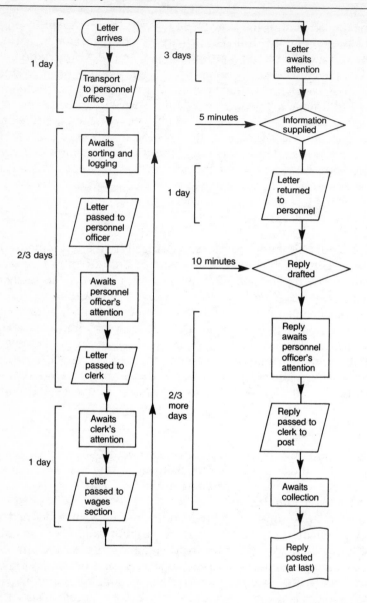

Figure 12 System delay in replying to routine correspondence

One day elapses between the arrival of the letter in the post room and it being transported to the Personnel Office. Another day passes before the letter is 'logged in' and placed on the personnel officer's desk, where it waits at least another day, as the personnel officer is out of the office a lot. The personnel officer then hands the letter to his clerk (each personnel officer is assigned a clerk). The next day, the clerk takes the letter to the wages department to obtain the requisite information. Since the wages department are busy working to weekly pay calculation deadlines, a further three days elapse before the wages clerk can take the five minutes required to look up the figure and scribble it on the letter. The letter then spends a day in the internal mail back to the personnel clerk. The personnel clerk then drafts a two-line reply which takes him about ten minutes. The draft letter next waits for another day or so on the Personnel Officer's desk to be checked and signed. The letter is then passed back to the clerk to post. Since the mail has already been collected, the envelope lies in the tray for one more day. Waiting time accounts for ten working days, whereas the time required to execute the task is about 15 minutes. The system is so wasteful, and yet so easy to improve. For example, 50 per cent of the delay could be eliminated just by routing the letter to the wages department in the first place. Note also the delays produced by over-control by the personnel officer. Why does the letter need to pass through the chain of command, and why does the personnel officer need to sign it? He cannot possibly know whether the information is correct unless he repeats the entire operation himself.

Machine supervision also counts as lost time. It can be reduced by:

- Sensors which alert an operative if something is wrong.
- Assigning an operative to a group of machines, instead of only one.
- Grouping machines which do not require human supervision.

A word of caution: while machine supervision does not add value, there are many forms of human attendance which do. For example, jewellers' shops tend to be generously staffed, to enable customers to receive unhurried attention. In seeking to eliminate waste it is important to differentiate between added value and non-added-value functions. Traditional cost-cutting exercises seldom make this distinction, and so often do more harm than good in the long run.

Movement

Every unnecessary movement means lost time. Whereas some organisations have invested in robotics to reduce costs, the Japanese approach is to try and eliminate the need for movement in the first place.[6] Identifying unnecessary movements can entail challenging long-held assumptions about what is the fastest way of doing things. For example, a factory worker's job was to seal batches of small boxes. When the boxes were sealed the practice was to load them *en masse* into a container, in order to minimise the amount of movement. In fact, this single movement was actually slower than placing each small box in the container separately, because of the difficulty of manoeuvring a large pile of small boxes into a confined space.

The reason many operations are inefficient is that they are based upon the idea that the task comes first, the person performing it second. This short-sighted approach explains why, for decades, operatives on car assembly lines had to bend and twist to work inside the engine compartment of a vehicle. Redesigning operations to fit the task to the person does not lead to sloth and anarchy. It speeds production by eliminating unproductive movement, reducing fatigue and the possibility of accidents.

Over-production

The Japanese aim to restrict production to immediate requirements. Storage space is deliberately limited and machines are stopped when buffer stocks reach a certain level. It is known as 'making today what is needed tomorrow', or 'just in time' production, which is described later in this chapter.

Rejects

Rejects result in delay somewhere in the system, hence the application of TQM principles.

Set-up times

Some of the most dramatic achievements of the Japanese concern reductions in set-up times, in some cases from five hours to three minutes. Figure 13 depicts the magnitude of this reduction.

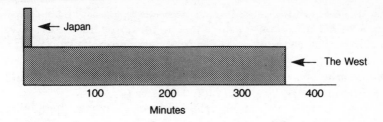

Figure 13 Japanese and Western set-up times compared

Reducing set-up times not only yields direct cost savings, but, most importantly, means that manufacturers can respond quickly and easily to changes in demand, and can offer customers a wider choice of goods.[7]

Reducing set-up times means being attuned to the concept of added value, and seeking out waste. A company garage, for example, used to service vehicles according to demand. It means that on any one day a variety of makes, ages and conditions would be dealt with – each requiring different equipment and materials to be assembled before it could be worked on. Streamlining operations, whereby all vehicles of one make were received on a particular day and all vehicles of another make were received on another day led to reduced set-up times and a faster turn-round. Obviously it meant that internal customers, ie supervisors, had to plan ahead. They soon discovered that this gentle discipline at least meant that they could be sure that a vehicle would be serviced that day, instead of being left indefinitely because parts were not available or staff just did not get round to dealing with them. Interestingly, forcing supervisors to think ahead enhanced the overall efficiency of operations. Not only were they more likely to have the vehicles they needed when they needed them, but planning one aspect of their operations forced them to plan the rest.

Transportation

Transportation means delay, be it moving components from one place to another, taking a meal from the kitchen to the table, or faxing a letter. Most manufacturing and service operations involve a whole series of delays. Imagine finishing light bulbs for example. One operative fixes attachments. A second operative then takes the assembled units and arranges them on a pallet. The pallets are then stored in a semi-finished area. A third operative then takes the pallets to assembly areas where they are processed automatically. A fourth operative then transfers the products to pallets which are lined up and transported to storage.[8] What proportion of expenditure of time and energy adds value?

A major cause of delay in value delivery systems is the human propensity to forget that the shortest distance between two points is a straight line. Simplification can substantially reduce the need for transportation by eliminating as many stages in a process as possible. London's emergency ambulance service is credited with the slowest response times in Britain. This is because under the existing manual system, the telephone operator first records the details. These are then passed to a control room to despatch clerks. The clerks then locate an ambulance from a manual file of available vehicles and then relay the message either to the ambulance by radio or by telephone to the local station. Assuming that the message is received and that the vehicle really is available, the ambulance crew must then thread their way through the traffic and lose further time assessing the casualty when they arrive. The delay then is twofold, ie transporting the message and then transporting the vehicle. The current reorganisation of the service seeks to apply the straight-line principle. The system consists of computerised screen control of vehicles updated every thirteen seconds; direct transmission of calls and information about the casualty to a terminal in the ambulance, and paramedics patrolling on motorcycle to provide rapid medical assistance at serious incidents. The flexibility created by the new system also reduces the need for ambulance stations – illustrating the interrelationship between quality, cost and time.[9]

Process waste

Any process which does not add value should be eliminated. Although this may seem obvious, it is surprising how often we do things simply because that is how we have always done them. For example, it is practice in many offices to record all incoming correspondence, for fear of something being lost. Quite apart from the fact that the records are often too vague to identify a particular item, the system should be such that correspondence cannot be lost. What use is it to be able to consult a ledger and confirm to a customer that his letter was definitely received on 20 September and subsequently definitely lost? Some processes which ostensibly add value may actually be wasteful. Staining softwood window-frames, for example, ostensibly adds value, though it is cheaper in the long run to use UPVc frames, which do not require preparatory treatment or maintenance.

Materials

Just as a good cook never wastes food, organisations must ensure that quality systems are designed to minimise loss from theft, deterioration in storage, poor handling, and so forth.

Communication

Communications are often the stimulus to action and informed decision-making. Misunderstandings result in delay and waste, including, most significantly, lost opportunities. Despite their importance, communications are usually taken for granted, instead of being something which needs to be worked at and managed almost as a science. Many Japanese companies appraise executives upon the clarity of their communications; some even require managers to work through a check-list before despatching a memorandum. If this sounds unrealistic, it should be remembered that 80 per cent of organisational communications concern routine matters, and therefore lend themselves to a degree of structuring. Training is also vital, as communication via the various media is a skill. It cannot be assumed that people know how to make themselves clear on the telephone or in writing.

Administration

Paperwork absorbs time. This explains why mail-order customers, for example, need to allow 28 days for delivery, when a shop can despatch goods the same afternoon. The shorter and simpler an organisation's administrative procedures, including decision-making processes, the less waste and potential for error. Large firms are particularly prone to administrative inefficiency, because their very size makes them feel vulnerable. They seek to compensate, therefore by *over-control.*

A branch office needs a fax machine. In order to obtain one, the branch manager must first raise an order, which then requires the signature of the head office manager. The order is then checked against budget by the finance department, which then passes it to the purchasing office. The purchasing office then processes a separate order – in their time. Yet what do these checks in the system achieve? If the branch manager is equipped with a budget and guidelines, surely he can be left accountable? All that is necessary is one order and one signature.

Unnecessary inspection is a major source of delay. For example, in some hair salons a qualified stylist has to check the apprentice's work. Not only does the customer have to wait an extra five or ten minutes while the apprentice locates the stylist, but the stylist has to break his concentration and leave his own customer waiting. Surely if the apprentice is sufficiently competent to undertake the task he can judge the results for himself, and seek advice if necessary?

Delays in doctors' surgeries can be reduced by allowing patients to book the time they need, instead of apportioning appointments into five or ten-minute slots. When this idea was first piloted in the UK, health service staff resisted it because it passed control from them to the patient. What if everyone started booking half-hour appointments? The objection is false, because the patient determines the length of the consultation anyway. Asking the patient to estimate the time he needs reduces unpredictability – the major source of delay. .

Untidiness
Look at the piles of paper in your office. How many of these have you consulted in the last week or fortnight? If you needed to refer to something, would you even be able to retrieve the information? Untidiness slows value-delivery systems. Delays occur as staff work their way round obstacles and lose time searching for tools, forms and so forth. Indeed, think of the countless hours lost rummaging desks, pockets and handbags for pens alone! The answer is not to impose rules requiring staff to tidy up periodically, but to recognise that *tidiness is a product of the system*, and to re-design the system accordingly. Orderly working procedures eliminate the need for periodic rearrangement, because they are by definition self-tidying, to say nothing of being generally more efficient anyway.

Bottlenecks
Study Figure 14 for a moment. What is the capacity of the system per hour?

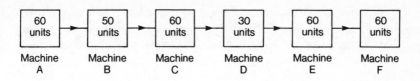

Figure 14 Process capacity per hour

The answer is 30, because *production is determined by the slowest stage in the process.* Moreover, actual production is lower than the theoretical maximum, because work tends to pile up at the bottleneck. Not only does the disruption result in delay, damage and therefore cost, but the secondary effects can be far-reaching if production must be rescheduled to meet commitments.

Bottlenecks are hardly unique to manufacturing organisations. The difference is that whereas in manufacturing the effects are obvious, *in service organisations bottlenecks are often invisible.*

Managers of service organisations are seldom engineers, and are therefore rarely attuned to the existence of bottlenecks, or their cost. Schooled in strict economy in all matters, they buy ten personal computers and only one printer, and wonder why things are even slower than they used to be. Likewise, a hospital X-ray department is only as fast as the slowest machine. Instead of trying to improve the system by investing in new or additional equipment, managers exhort staff to 'work round' monstrous and demotivating difficulties. This is short-sighted and lazy thinking, for not only does additional investment pay for itself, it almost invariably leads to substantial increases in productivity.

An hour lost at a bottleneck is an hour lost in the entire system.

Timing

Speed demands careful attention to logistics. According to Shingo, *delays are less about shortage of time and more about the effect of timing.*[10] In other words, when something is not done on time, it usually really means it was not done with proper timing. A major reason for untimeliness is sequential thinking. Managers are taught that a logical approach means proceeding step by step – moving only to the next operation when the previous one has been completed. The problem with this approach is that there are often substantial unavoidable delays between stages. Much time can be saved by structuring activities concurrently, ie identifying tasks which can be carried out simultaneously. In dentistry, for example, one patient receives local anaesthetic and while the anaesthetic takes effect, a second patient is treated. Although concurrent planning is a staple technique of project management, it has yet to find its way into the consciousness of many general managers and professions other than dentistry.

'JUST IN TIME' PRODUCTION

The JIT goal

Leading Japanese companies attribute their success in reducing waste and speeding production to the implementation of so-called 'just in time' (hereafter referred to as JIT) methods of working. JIT is a system which aims:

> [to] produce and deliver finished goods just in time to be sold, sub-assemblies just in time to be assembled into finished goods, fabricated parts just in time to go into sub-assemblies, and purchased materials just in time to be transformed into fabricated parts.[11]

REVERSING CONCEPTS

JIT production reverses conventional approaches to manufacturing, ie:

1. First sell it, then make it.

2. Production is planned backwards instead of forwards.

3. 'Pull' instead of 'push' systems of production.

Sell it then make it

Whereas the conventional approach to manufacturing is make it and then sell it, the JIT aim is the reverse: sell it and then make it.

Ideally nothing is produced until a customer is identified. This eliminates the need for warehousing and other costs of holding stock. In some Japanese factories, cars are shipped with the customer's name already attached.[12] Although some British manufacturers make to order, the speed of their operations is seldom competitive. Customers requiring office furniture, for example, must compose themselves in patience as delivery takes about eight weeks. In Japan, waiting time is eight days or less.

Think backwards

Whereas conventional mass production is planned from start to finish, *JIT begins with visualising the production process backwards.*

Under JIT, staff responsible for the final operation receive the production plan first. They determine their needs and then pass the plan backwards. The benefits of this approach are, first, that it overcomes the 'over the wall' mentality. Second, it facilitates clarity and rigour, as the organisation is forced to get the process right before commencing production. A good way to understand the power of this technique is to imagine a simple task such as tidying a room. To begin with, what does a tidy room look like? This question immediately creates a picture and defines the standard. Dusting might be the last operation because all the preceding ones raise it – what does that require and what precedes it? Anyone with sufficient mental discipline to pursue this idea to the first process (removing the old newspapers) will discover the potential of speed combined with direction.

'Pull' instead of 'push'

Conventional mass production is based on push,
whereas JIT production is based on pull.

Conventional production is known as a 'push' system because components flow along a conveyor to the operative, who processes these as they pass. For example, he might decorate cakes with a cherry, place the top on to pens, or pack tins into boxes. Production is dictated by the speed of the conveyor belt. Although the belt can be stopped in an emergency, the idea is that the operative must keep pace with production.

Conventional systems have the advantage of predictability, which enables the application of sophisticated mathematical techniques of optimising production. The price is inflexibility, as conventional systems require long production runs. Since changeover is cumbersome and costly, it is difficult to cope with frequent or sudden variations in demand. Further, intricate balancing is necessary to maintain a steady flow. Since such precision can rarely be achieved, each stage of the process must be protected by buffer stocks, with all the attendant costs. The indirect costs of stock are high; for example, work in progress can occupy up to 70 per cent of the floor-space of a factory.

Pull-based production systems are designed to eliminate stock and facilitate flexibility. They are based upon backwards thinking, and operative control. The idea is that nothing passes down the line until the operative is ready to receive it. Readiness is signalled by the operative literally pulling the components towards his work station. Theoretically, stock cannot accumulate because everything is produced 'just in time' for the next operation.

A further advantage of pull systems is a *reduced probability of defects*. If an operative 'pulls down' a defect, it cannot be ignored as there is no replacement. Further, the person responsible for the defect is readily identifiable and receives immediate feedback, because the process stops.

REORGANISING FOR JIT

Implementing JIT systems requires radical reorganisation, the intricacies of which are beyond the scope of this book. The basic principle, however, is simple. Whereas conventional systems are like mass armies – huge, expensive and rigid – JIT is a guerrilla method of production – small, cheap and flexible. The features of JIT production include:

■ Numerous small machines.
■ Spare capacity.
■ Small batch production.
■ Employee flexibility.
■ Managerial involvement in engineering technicalities.
■ Employee responsibility for maintaining production.
■ Preventive maintenance.
■ 'Just in time' supplies.

Small machines

Conventional production systems use large, complex machines designed for speed and long production runs. JIT uses numerous, small, inexpensive and adaptable machines to enable quick change-over and manufacture of a variety of products. Machine layout and materials handling must also be reorganised accordingly.

Spare capacity

Traditional mass production must be geared to full capacity in order to optimise the use of expensive plant and equipment. JIT systems operate well below full capacity in order to maintain flexibility. They are able to do so because the benefits of responsiveness are substantially greater than the cost of a few small inexpensive machines standing idle.

Small batch production

Whereas traditional manufacturing is based upon achieving economies of scale, JIT seeks to reap the benefits of flexibility by producing goods only in response to demand. Small batch production and fast set-up times enable manufacturers to switch production rapidly. This enables them to respond to changes in demand and reduces the likelihood of over-production and the need to carry stock.

Reducing batch sizes improves productivity

A relationship exists between batch size and total production time. For example, a manufacturer who halved batch sizes found that production time decreased by 65 per cent.[13]

Employee flexibility

With conventional mass production, staff wait for the work to arrive. JIT is based upon the opposite principle, requiring the staff to go to the work. Staff move around the shop-floor undertaking a variety of functions according to process demands. If a breakdown occurs, staff help one another or move to other work. Once production targets are achieved, work ceases. Staff either carry out maintenance duties or, if no other work is available, are sent home.

Managerial involvement in production engineering

Few Western general managers see it as their role to become involved in the design, commissioning and repair of plant and machinery. JIT demands such involvement in technicalities, because an important part of management's responsibility is keeping the system going and ensuring that daily targets are met.

Employee responsibility

In my last organisation, a decree was passed requiring all machinery repairs to be referred to the central work shop. Consequently, if a light bulb failed on a van, the vehicle had to be transported 16 miles and wait for anything from 24 hours to ten days for attention. JIT works on the opposite principle. Shop-floor operatives deal with as many production problems as possible themselves, including repairs. The rationale is that time spent waiting for the engineer is time wasted; and besides, in 80 per cent of breakdowns, machines can be rectified without specialist attention.

Preventive maintenance

Stockless production can ill-afford breakdowns. Preventive maintenance therefore forms an important part of JIT systems. Reducing the probability of machine failure begins with purchasing of good tools and equipment. Cheap tools are a false economy. Not only are they unpleasant and a hindrance to work with, they actually inflict damage during their (mercifully) short lives.[14]

Although routine maintenance is a feature of all manufacturing plants it tends to be a fairly passive exercise. JIT pushes the function to the forefront of managerial attention. A feature of JIT is proactive system maintenance, sometimes called 'total preventive maintenance'. In some plants, operatives are responsible for routine servicing.

'Just in time' supplies

The advantages of single-source purchasing were explained in chapter 2. Two other JIT ideals are:

■ the organisation of suppliers to deliver small lots frequently to the point of use;
■ the absence of receiving inspections.

The elimination of stock requires frequent deliveries of small quantities, exactly packaged, 'just in time' for production. Since transportation entails cost, delivery is ideally to the point of processing.

Receiving inspections are a cost, and add no value. The aim of JIT is to eliminate the need for these by working with the supplier to ensure that his systems are capable of meeting requirements, and that these requirements are understood.

THE ACHILLES' HEEL OF JIT

Stockless production leaves organisations extremely vulnerable to:

■ supply failures;
■ the effects of industrial action.

Potential supply failures

In practice, many organisations, including leading Japanese firms, have failed to develop the relationship with their suppliers which Deming argues is essential to quality. Suppliers typically resent what they perceive as interference in their organisations, particularly when accompanied by ruthless price bargaining. Suppliers see themselves as bearing the cost of delivery to the point of use at 15-minute intervals. Further, many British JIT systems are far from perfect. Suppliers often feel they are bearing the brunt of 'half-baked' schemes.[15] These tensions suggest that the potential for supply failure is high.

Vulnerability to industrial action

JIT has been implemented by force in some firms.[16, 17, 18] The consequences of coercion, and the alternatives, are discussed in detail in chapter 8. Here it is sufficient to say that organisations may well be sowing the seeds of conflict where they can least afford it. The paucity of buffer stocks gives the workforce the potential to halt production at little cost to themselves.[19]

SUMMARY

■ Time is now an important competitive weapon.
■ Performance improvement results in reduced cost and greater flexibility.
■ Operations may be classified as those which add value and those which do not.
■ The key to time-based competition is the elimination of waste.
■ Waste is any operation which does not add value.
■ Many Western practices are extremely inefficient; over 99 per cent of the time spent on some operations adds no value to the product or service.
■ Sources of waste include:

- tentative placement;
- waiting time;
- unnecessary movement;
- over-production;
- rejects;
- set-up times;
- transportation;
- process waste;
- materials waste;
- communication;
- administration;
- untidiness;
- bottlenecks;
- bad timing.

■ JIT is a goal based upon the elimination of waste.
■ JIT is sometimes known as stockless production, because the aim is to receive supplies and manufacture components 'just in time' for the next operation.
■ JIT production reverses conventional approaches to manufacturing, ie:

- sell it, then make it;
- production planned backwards instead of forwards;
- 'pull' instead of 'push' systems of production.

■ The features of JIT production include:

- numerous small machines;
- spare capacity;
- small batch production;
- employee flexibility;
- managerial involvement in engineering technicalities;
- employee responsibility for maintaining production;
- preventive maintenance;
- 'just in time' supplies.

■ Stockless production is extremely vulnerable to supply failures and industrial action.

8

BUILDING A QUALITY CULTURE

A country, or a village or a community, cannot be developed; it can only develop itself. For real development means the development, the growth, of people. Every country in Africa can show examples of modern facilities which have been provided for the people . . . and which are now rotting unused. We have schools, irrigation works, expensive markets and so on . . . things by which someone came and tried to 'bring development to the people'. If real development is to take place, the people have to be involved . . . for the truth is that development means the development of the *people*. Roads, buildings, the increase of crop output, and many other things of this nature are not development; they are only tools of development. A new road extends man's freedom only if he travels upon it.[1]

'ROTTING UNUSED'

Creating a new organisational culture is the Western world's opportunity to beat Japanese competition. The opportunity will be lost if organisations opt for shortcuts. For 'schools, irrigation works', and 'expensive markets' read 'better communications, mission statements and notices hung on people's walls' – today's trappings of easy excellence, tomorrow's 'rotting unused'.

If this assertion seems pessimistic, remember how quality circles were hailed as 'The most exciting and profound approach to management to have become established in the world since the advent of "scientific management".'[2] What are quality circles now if not 'rotting unused'?

Quality circles failed because they were 'tools of development'.

which organisations used to foster their objectives without developing either the people or the organisational infra-structure to support them.[3] TQM will become the next 'rotting unused' if organisations try to implement the techniques without a fundamental change in 'the way we do things'.

Not too late

Much has been said about Japanese advances in quality and production efficiency. While these advances are highly significant it is not too late for other countries to begin development. Japanese industry has problems of its own. Although Japanese workers are portrayed as sublimely co-operative, industrious and group orientated, the management system is basically coercive. Workers are expected to forgo part of their holiday entitlement and to work long hours. Pay is dependent upon exhibiting the 'right' attitudes. Quality circles are a source of pressure as individuals' suggestion rates are publicly displayed. Individuals perceive themselves as perpetually under pressure to agree with their supervisors.[4, 5, 6]

Although it is worth studying Japanese production techniques, the benefits of emulating their human relations policies are doubtful. Coercion destroys involvement – the very thing which TQM seeks to create. Research indicates that the Japanese have achieved success at a price. The price is high levels of tension at work and job-related stress. Beneath the stereotype, Japanese workers actually experience less job satisfaction and pleasure in work than their Western counterparts. Their commitment to the organisation too is comparatively low.[7, 8] Unsurprisingly, Japanese workers are beginning to question their conditions of employment.

This presents the Western world with a potential lead. Japanese quality systems assume conventional power structures and cultures including a clear division between managers and the managed. While these are workable, to a point, in the long term, TQM demands a radically different approach to organisation. The problem facing Japan is that having come so far in a particular direction, there may be little alternative but to continue with existing frameworks, even though these are already under strain.

The comparative under-development of Western organisations is an advantage because they possess much greater scope for change. Improvement of quality and the development of an appropriate organisational culture can proceed hand in hand. Since each re-enforces the other, the resultant synergistic potential could result in improvements happening faster and being more dramatic than anyone might otherwise dare to predict.

THE NEW INDUSTRIAL REVOLUTION

It was suggested in chapter 1 that TQM is a means to an end. The end is continued viability through the development of a quality culture as distinct from a profit culture. This is not to suggest that profits are insignificant; far from it. The difference, however, between conventional ways of 'doing things' and TQM, is that TQM requires organisations to take a lateral view of profits. Whereas conventional management stresses maximum quantity for least cost, TQM is devoted to the production of quality goods and services.

It is counter-productive to try and bolt a quality culture on to systems and practices which are orientated to maximising short-term profits, as doing so only creates contradictions. A fresh approach is required. What follows is not a blue-print for trans-formation or 'ten easy steps' to building a new culture. It is an attempt to set aside out-dated assumptions and practices and to explore the implications of the so-called 'quality revolution'.

Second order change: the key to cultural transformation

There are basically two types of change ie:

1. first order change, and,

2. second order change.

First order change is change within the system, ie more of the same. Second order change is change which changes the system.[9] Building a quality culture requires a second order change. The biggest impediment to advancement is seldom the problem itself, but the assumptions made about the problem. Shedding assump-tions frees us to think of other possibilities.[10]

Conventional management is riveted to 'the problem' of man-aging people. If we redefine 'the problem' as how to produce quality goods and services, then we can change our thinking from 'the problem' of managing people to 'the potential' of people managing.

Whereas conventional management stresses human resource management, building a quality culture is about developing resourceful humans to enable *them* to manage.

The progression consists of a gradual change in emphasis which moves through three phases. These are:

1. human resource management;

2. managing and developing resourceful humans; and

3. resourceful humans managing.

The key to development is to set in motion a virtuous circle. The virtuous circle consists of developing the organisation in a manner which simultaneously develops the people which further enables the people to develop the organisation.

SUSTAINABLE DEVELOPMENT: THE STARTING POINT

Building a quality culture involves ambitious innovations in training, employee participation and so forth. The reader may feel that some of the ideas described in this book, such as Deming's views on education and training, however appealing are financial suicide. Indeed, some motor companies have already abandoned the elaborate employee selection techniques used by their Japanese counterparts as too expensive. Does this mean we are defeated before we even start?

Surely organisations have forgotten to ask what they need such innovations for. The Japanese need to recruit conformists – hence the careful screening. A second order approach is to recruit people to develop the organisation and themselves simultaneously, rather than take the organisation as an inflexible entity and to try and match people to it.

Organisations need to be realistic and they need to start somewhere. The concept of *sustainable development* provides a useful basis for planning change. Sustainable development is development which meets the needs of the present without compromising the organisation's ability to meet future needs. Although the criterion for sustainability is change within existing organisational capability, sustainable development is a dynamic process, because change enhances capability and so generates resources for further development.

Bringing existing cultures under control

Improvement starts with bringing existing processes under control. Control in this context means consistency between an organisation's stated objectives and actual practice. Without consistency, employees do not know what to believe. For instance, how can a hospital trust talking about 'putting patients first' when doctors refer to patients as 'punters'? Likewise:

> When they ask you why you want to be an investment banker, you're supposed to talk about the challenges, and the thrill of doing deals, and the excitement of working with such high calibre people, but never, ever mention money.

> Learning a new lie was easy. Believing it was another matter .... That money wasn't the binding force was, of course, complete and utter bullshit.[11]

Inconsistency results in schizophrenia. An example of schizophrenia is publicising customer service and then reprimanding employees who replace allegedly faulty goods for wasting money.

The costs of inconsistency are high. This is because conflict is resolved in the direction of greatest attraction. Faced with a dilemma between public concern for quality and private concern for short-term profits, employees will opt for the course of action promising greatest reward or least risk to themselves. Consequently every move towards progress is actually regressive. Instead of capitalising upon the opportunity to impress a customer, employees do the opposite. Inconsistency results in 'one step forward, three back'.

Managing for consistency

It need not require huge resources to bring a measure of consistency to the organisation but nor will this happen by accident. Consistency, like process control, must be managed and watched continuously. Creating cultural consistency is basically a balancing act between what the organisation would like to be and what it really is. Good intentions are counterproductive if they merely raise false expectations. For example:

> Treat people as adults. Treat them as partners; treat them with dignity; treat them with respect . . . . If you want productivity and the financial reward that goes with it, you must treat workers as your most important asset.[12]

This is an example of change within the system which is actually detrimental because it is only skin deep. The concept of treating people as partners may be laudable, but partners in what? Partnership implies an equal share of power in the running of the organisation and distribution of profits. Is that really feasible? Besides, if an employee is a partner how can he simultaneously be an asset? Partnership implies equality whereas an asset is something that is owned, used and disposable. Organisations can best command credibility by being realistic with employees.

The most powerful change agent in creating consistency is managerial will. The motto for effectiveness is *deeds not words*.

It may be necessary to forbid inappropriate language, but only leadership by example will convince employees of the organisation's sincerity. Likewise, organisational sentiments about precious human resources are just so many empty words. It is the creation of single status facilities, upgrading of mess rooms and so forth which demonstrate commitment. If action is impractical either adopt a more realistic tone or, dispense with the rhetoric altogether. Employees will not miss it. Besides who are you trying to convince, them or yourself?

Contradictions are inevitable in a developing organisation. They become harmful only if they remain unresolved. Again, managerial will is the key to creating an atmosphere conducive to airing disagreement, and it is similarly important that the mechanisms exist for doing so. Part of the function of employee involvement is to identify and rectify inconsistency.

It may be useful to devise a set of organisational principles as a framework for resolving contradictions. The value of such guiding principles is that they provide a bedrock of clarity in a changing environment, but unlike rules and regulations, are sufficiently flexible to prevent the development of anomalies.

Room for improvement

Although TQM involves careful planning and structuring, any improvement is progressive provided it is sustainable. Having achieved a reasonable degree of consistency, organisations should then do the obvious first, ie concentrate upon changes which *add greatest value for least cost*. A restaurant, for example, may achieve a significant improvement at no cost by changing its meat supplier. A hotel may attract new custom for a relatively small additional cost by providing answerphones in every room.

The danger is the temptation to continue to look for quick success which then degenerates into the trappings of quality. Management by walking about, for example, will only take an organisation so far. Deep and lasting change requires rigorous attention to the production system and working with people to improve it.

Building the foundations

An excellent way to begin more systematic development is to focus upon improving process capability by:

■ examining existing systems and procedures, and,
■ improving these.

Change can be easy. Localised improvements such as reducing delays in the distribution of mail, improving information access and storage and providing extra customer facilities are simple to enact and they all add up.

The most significant benefit of making a start in this way is the effect upon morale. This 'hands on' approach represents second order change because it results in shared responsibility for change instead of change being something which is imposed by management. Commitment and cohesion are created because process development:

1. involves employees in managing;

2. forces managers to recognise the difficulties employees work under;

3. demonstrates management's commitment to quality by deed rather than words, and

4.   actually results in change.

Unlike the rise and fall of quality campaigns, such subtle change is fruitful and lasting. The improvements may be modest. Most important is the mutual confidence generated by the new style of working. The school leaver who finds his suggestions for reducing paperwork taken seriously is never the same person again. The manager who sees for the first time just how hard his staff have to work reaches a new and irrevocable level of understanding. Success begets success. To build trust, confidence, and insight is to generate resources for further development.

DEVELOPING THE POTENTIAL

The next stage is to capitalise upon potential. Once employees see that change is possible, and that they and not the management are the primary agents of development, the impetus for further improvement exists.

A new approach to setting standards

Second order change is often counter-intuitive. Standards are central to quality. The intuitive approach to managing production and services, therefore, is to compile detailed specifications and enforce these rigorously. The problems with this method are:

■ It is conducive to failure.
■ Effective supervision is difficult.
■ Management's role is reduced to one of policing.

The more detailed the specifications the easier it is for an employee to make a mistake because his concentration is thinly spread instead of being focused upon essentials. Developmental activities are neglected since management's attention is wholly absorbed in inspection. Yet effective inspection is impossible because management's attention is likewise dissipated by the plethora of items.

It is better to emulate the designer's credo and instead of imposing tight tolerances which are difficult to enforce aim for: *loose tolerances, tightly enforced* (see page 48). Employees need guidance and the security of knowing that slip-shod work will be rejected. Equally they need room to develop their own style of working and to think about what they are doing and how it could be improved. Clearly there are some occupations (laboratory testing, for example) where it is necessary to insist upon specific tolerances. In the majority of occupations it is not. Craftsmen, for example, have no difficulty in working to parameters such as 'neat and tidy', 'leave in a workman-like state', and 'good workmanship'.

Tight tolerances set a ceiling upon achievement and are therefore a barrier to improvement. Loose tolerances enable employees to exceed expectations. Part of the purpose of the exercise is to stimulate employee suggestions such as 'can't we get rid of x', and 'why can't we do y?'. The challenge to management is to channel efforts systematically without de-motivating employees or creating a lumbering bureaucracy for the tortuous processing of suggestions. It is a challenge which cannot be over-estimated because it means a significant departure from the concept of managers as controllers to that of facilitators.

Breaking With tradition

Systems improvement and the creation of flexible frameworks are only the start. The next step is to set aside taken-for-granted assumptions about human motivation and see what possibilities that creates. Conventional management is based on a negative view of motivation emanating from the early days of industrialisation when agricultural labour proved reluctant to submit to factory rules.[13]

This historical legacy continues to inform management thinking and research. We study motivation because we assume motivation is problematic. This assumption prevents us from seeing that most people, given a job reasonably consistent with their abilities and aspirations, are motivated. It is their organisational experiences which de-motivate them. What happens, for example, to the motivation of a young recruit who learns that policing is about keeping the figures looking good – forget the sworn duty of protecting the community? What happens to the motivation of a garage apprentice who learns that 'service' means doing the bare minimum and sometimes cutting corners?

TQM views motivation like the growth potential of a plant. Provided the sapling is tended and nurtured, it will develop. The role of management is to see that it is gently trained in a productive direction and protected from the deprivations which would otherwise destroy it.

Employees as standard setters

A positive view of motivation is the foundation for a new approach to improving quality. Standard setting is a managerial function because a negative view of motivation suggests that employees are interested in restricting the quantity and quality of output. We further assume, therefore, that it is necessary for managers to set standards. This assumption prevents us from seeing that *employee standards may be higher than managerial standards.*

Imagine a doctor's surgery. Management might set standards as follows:

Check-list for receptionists

1. Patients to be greeted by 'hello' followed by their name.

2. Check patient's address.

3. Patient to be notified if doctor is running more than 20 minutes late.

4. Patient asked to take a seat.

5. When patient leaves, check whether a repeat appointment is necessary.

6. Say 'good-bye' to patient.

Note: Staff are strictly forbidden to discuss clinical matters with patients.

Staff might well view these instructions as an insult. Not only do they greet patients courteously but they always try and take a little time to engage in social chat as many patients are elderly and live alone. On the issue of delay, staff might say there would be fewer hold-ups if consultations were not interrupted by doctors telephoning hospitals for test results – a task which receptionists could perform in advance if the doctors would only co-operate. As regards the warning at the end of the check-list, staff might point out that they are sufficiently knowledgeable and trustworthy to check prescription details and offer general support and advice without compromising clinical judgement. Further, with appropriate training and encouragement, they could do considerably more.

Target setting

Management by targets is another aspect of standard setting which is typically counterproductive. Although the purpose of targets is to galvanise people into action, the effect may be the opposite, in that *targets limit achievement.*

Although people may enjoy working to and beating realistic targets, they might very well define more ambitious objectives for themselves than any management would dare impose. Although in theory targets are negotiable, in practice they are often unrealistic and irrelevant and have an adverse effect upon quality. Edicts such as, 'All stocks to be eliminated within six months' produce results, ie not an item of stock in sight. All that will have happened, however, is that an outside organisation will be being paid to hold stocks on the organisation's behalf and the expense concealed in the accounts.[14]

Managers as enablers

Whereas traditional management emphasises control and imposition in setting standards, in a quality culture the role of managers will be to provide the forum for employees to address priorities and work upon improvements.

Quality is a product of the system. Instead of focusing upon ostensible outcomes, such as a 5 per cent increase in sales, managers will need to concentrate upon the processes whereby results are achieved. It will no longer be good enough, if it ever was, for managers to merely issue demands for performance. A major part of a manager's role in a quality culture will be to work in a 'hands on' fashion with employees, continuously identifying new directions and the means of accomplishing change.

The separation of conception from execution is a wasteful arrogance. Employees have a role to play in planning and improvement. The reason employee participation has such a dismal history is that it is typically approached in a first order manner as a managerial concession – something which counts as unproductive time. Organisations are prevented from progressing beyond first order change because of fixed assumptions about the role of managers *vis à vis* that of employees, ie managers manage and employees obey.

Participation in a quality culture requires a more sophisticated model, whereby organisations abandon the traditional demarcation between managers and the managed and instead recognise that *all employees will need to assume some managerial responsibility*. Job descriptions at all levels will need to incorporate specific responsibility for attendance at production and quality meetings. Employees will, as part of their job, be required to contribute information and ideas and comment critically upon issues – responsibilities which will be reflected in their remuneration. The role of management will be to stimulate ideas and to shape the process.

Enabling managers

New styles of working can only become a reality if properly resourced. This in turn requires organisations to abandon the culture of minimising short-term cost. Minimisation involves the manager in perpetual politicking and corner fighting – the very things which TQM seeks to breed out of organisations. Resources may be scarce but our misplaced assumptions about what constitutes good management make them scarcer. How does it serve organisations when managers are perpetually preoccupied with the problem of how to procure a dollar and then make it do the work of two? How does it benefit quality when the system guarantees that resources are allocated to the politically skilled rather than those who need them?

A second order change involves abandoning the assumption that least is best, and instead asking *what is needed*? Arguably this is precisely what good management involves. The problem is that, in practice, a profit culture encourages people to take short cuts, ostensibly in the interests of efficiency. For example, a manager asks for 50 machines. The order is automatically pruned to 45 – why? In a quality culture the managerial imperative is not how to make do, but *to do*.

This will call for the development of new skills. Hitherto managers have been so preoccupied with fighting for resources that acquisition has become an end in itself. Managers will need to build expertise in identifying what resources are needed for various initiatives and in deploying these. This is by no means as simple as it sounds. A major aspect of managerial work in a quality culture will concern multi-disciplinary teams. Bringing and welding such expertise together in a complex organisation will be no mean feat of accomplishment.

DEVELOPING PEOPLE

Discarding old assumptions about efficiency

One of the biggest obstacles to improving quality is de-skilling. The logic of de-skilling is that the less skill a task entails, the cheaper it becomes. The more tasks which can be de-skilled therefore, the cheaper the operation. De-skilling is reflected in the repetitive work and narrowly defined roles of many production line operatives. De-skilling is also evident in service organisations. For example, cook-chill technology, whereby meals are prepared at a central location and then regenerated on site, aims to minimise the number of skilled chefs required.

De-skilling is inappropriate in a quality culture because it results in waste through

- insufficient training;
- jobs being wrongly perceived as requiring no skill;
- the alienation of both customer and employee.

In a profit culture the only training which is justified is that which is strictly necessary to enable an employee to do his job. In practice this seldom amounts to more than communicating instructions. For instance, 'training' someone to answer the telephone in a set way is not training at all. The employee is not learning anything except what management wants him to say. This explains why so many employees in service organisations are devoid of even basic product knowledge.

De-skilling obscures the fact that many so-called routine jobs require considerable skill. A customer once returned a recording of a violin concerto to the shop complaining it was a bad pressing. The shop assistant listened to the record. 'You are right,' he said,

'So and So doesn't play like that.' How many counter staff are trained to this level? Receptionists in estate agents' offices perform what are regarded as routine tasks, such as distributing sales literature, making viewing appointments and so forth. Few organisations recognise that receptionists are central to negotiations activity, ideally placed to observe bargaining signals and often confronted with delicate situations. Quite apart from the risks of a deal being wrecked, it cuts a very poor impression when the receptionist has to pass the client to someone in authority. Why not capitalise upon the receptionist's potential and train him in negotiation behaviour?

Part of the rationale of de-skilling is to automate tasks which would otherwise involve the exercise of judgement. Whereas supplicants for credit, for instance, were once interviewed by the bank manager, nowadays they speak with a clerk in the 'machine room' who works through a check-list parrot fashion. De-skilling alienates both employee and customer. It alienates employees because it reduces them to robots approving applications which meet the criteria and referring to higher authority those which do not. The customer is alienated because he knows the person he is dealing with has no discretion. Should a problem arise, he will be passed to an assistant manager with the power to say 'no' but not the power to say 'yes'. He may not even be allowed to speak with the manager.

The rationale for de-skilling is efficiency. Yet organisations are already beginning to perceive that de-skilling is often wasteful. When a machine breaks down, for example, operatives send for the engineer because 'it's his problem'. When a query arises in an office, a client is delayed while the manager is summoned, 'I could deal with it', says the clerk, 'but I'm not allowed to'.

Some manufacturers have devolved responsibility for maintenance and minor repairs to the workforce only to make things worse:

> Employees are not merely encouraged but *expected* to identify process problems, intervene in production, rectify them and suggest changes in the organisation of production to prevent their reoccurence. Far from . . . improving the quality of working life, this widening of responsibility creates extra stress and makes the experience of work 'more precarious'.[15]

This is an example of a first order change whereby management have taken the shortcut of merely adding to employee's roles without proper training, remuneration or revising the whole concept of their employment. Not only is the system strained, but, most seriously, management have destroyed the credibility required to implement second order change.

A second order approach to re-skilling

Conventional management minimises potential, whereas second order change seeks to maximise it.

In a profit culture when we speak of maximising resources what we really mean is loading more on to people. For instance, we maximise the use of a receptionist by adding responsibility for petty cash, car parking and so on.

Second order thinking in a quality culture seeks development through increased responsibility and training. A useful starting point is *how might this role serve the customer?* A playground assistant in a school, for example, is in a prime position to observe behaviour and to contribute to learning and development. He can only do so if properly trained and integrated into the school's management structure.

Sustainable development

Sustainable development in training starts with the basics. A telephonist, for example, might learn about voice projection and other techniques of using the telephone to inspire confidence. An assistant in a pen shop might learn about the capability and specification of the various writing instruments on sale and customers' needs for attention. Training staff in the basics improves the product or service and establishes individual confidence. Together they create the resources for further development.

Part of the basics includes training for involvement. Organisations must recognise that decades of conditioning and repression cannot be changed by 'from now on everything is going to be different' speeches. Calling staff into *ad hoc* meetings and asking them to say what they think is precisely the sort of behaviour which results in blank stares and embarrassed silence as both parties conclude that the exercise is a waste of time. Just as employees need to be trained to operate machinery, they need to be trained and educated to develop the problem-solving skills, confidence and articulation to enable them to contribute meaningfully. Innovations such as showing new manufacturing designs to employees have yielded encouraging results. The function of training and structural development is to transform 'ad hocery' into a systematic and powerful technique of management.

Beyond the basics

The aim of training and education must be to enable employees to realise their potential as part of a continuous improvement strategy. This means equipping employees to go beyond their initial role prescription. Some solicitors, for example, train their clerks to interview witnesses and attend clients in police stations. The investment is extremely profitable. It enhances staff job satisfaction and enables staff to see the relevance of the more routine aspects of their work. It creates flexibility, thus enabling practices to acquire business which would otherwise be lost. Not least, it generates income and hence the resources for further development.

Organisations need to look at the potential locked up in supposedly routine jobs and ask themselves *why not?* Why not train the garage receptionist to handle sales and/or carry out repairs? Why not train the museum attendant to conduct tours and give talks? Why not train the personnel clerk to help out with interviews? The reader may say, 'We do that already.' Good, so why not approach it systematically as part of a continuous improvement strategy?

Managing the learning organisation

Again, the challenge to management should not be under-estimated. Although much has been written about managing turbulent environments, the management of people is rooted in the concept of managers as controllers whose aim is to achieve order and stability. A quality culture will demand managers capable of maintaining a dynamic equilibrium in which everyone understands what they are doing yet roles are constantly developing.

WILL ORGANISATIONS STILL NEED MANAGERS?

Management as we know it will eventually cease to exist. There are two reasons for this prediction. First, managerial functions such as controlling, scheduling and inspection are non-value-adding activities. Organisations will therefore seek to eliminate these just as they are currently trying to eliminate transportation, positioning, movement and other forms of waste. After all, what the customer cares about is the price and quality of his software, his holiday, his car etc, not the fact that it took sixteen MBAs working fourteen hours a day, seven days a week, to produce it.

Second, re-skilling will enable responsibility for such managerial functions as cannot be eliminated to be devolved upon employees. Control and supervision are non-value-adding activities. Individuals in organisations will therefore become increasingly self-regulating. Hierarchical structures will become redundant to be replaced by overlapping 'spheres of influence'.

Leadership in the sense of negotiator, facilitator, resource procurer and figurehead will be necessary but leading will no longer be the prerogative of a managerial elite. Leaders will be democratically elected, as already happens in some university departments. Given a better educated, better skilled, more confident workforce, who is better equipped to lead?

The quality of working life

This book has moved from the notion of quality as a means to organisational survival and prosperity to the precursor of a new industrial era. While it would be misleading to paint a picture of Utopia, logically continuous improvement surely has positive implications for the quality of working life?

Improvement in the quality of working life will flow from a second order change from the concept of labour as a commodity to the recognition that labour *is* the organisation. The evidence of a link between quality production and quality of working life can already be seen in firms noted for their enlightened human resource management policies, such as Hewlett-Packard.

The development of a quality culture will take such policies further – to a point where conventional management philosophy seems like folklore. Again, the vehicle for change is the concept of sustainable development which generates its own momentum. There is evidence that re-skilling even on a modest scale, supported by proper training, increases job satisfaction and reduces stress.[16] Such change fulfils two purposes. First, it enables the organisation to become more efficient without de-stabilising it. Second, it creates trust and an enhanced sense of meaning in work. Either of these factors provides a solid basis for development. Their combined force, however, is potentially formidable.

In time, the worst effects of occupational stress are likely to be eradicated as organisations recognise the need to calculate the total cost of decisions concerning workplace facilities and practices. For example, open plan offices are designed to minimise expenditure on rent. Yet what is the real cost when the consequences of noise, disturbance and lack of privacy are taken into account? First order changes such as erecting extra screens and notices asking employees to keep the noise down are not the answer. The answer is a second order change which takes as its starting point the question of what conditions are conducive to high quality work.

In future, negative experiences of work, such as stress and demotivation, will be regarded as seriously as an outbreak of cholera. (If this seems an exaggeration, remember that a hundred and fifty years ago, epidemics were a fact of life.) Two things will happen. First, organisations will wake up to the consequences of psychological debilitation. Second, organisations will discover that, like cholera, such epidemics are controllable.

Control requires a second order change. Approaches such as pep talks and performance appraisal are like vaccinations, ie they are first order changes. What is needed is the development of an organisational infrastructure conducive to psychological health, just as good sanitation and pure water supplies and the like are the key to the eradication of disease. Again, progress is likely to be exponential. Preventing demotivation, for example, far from resulting in a static state, will actually release energy as individuals perceive the freedom to realise their potential.

The quality of life

The foregoing pages have barely scratched the surface of the possibilities implicit in the new industrial revolution. Freedom from the shackles of the last industrial revolution will enable organisations to develop as communities serving the greater community. And serve they shall. For as society increasingly reaps the harvest of the so-called quality movement, it is all the more likely to insist upon what is basically justice, ie sound and robust goods in exchange for precious coinage. As for the purveyor of goods or services found wanting, he shall be immediately sent for . . .

SUMMARY

■ Creating a quality culture is the key to beating competition from the Japanese.
■ Japanese improvements in quality have been achieved under a coercive culture which is now strained.
■ The comparative under-development of Western organisations is an advantage.
■ The creation of a quality culture requires organisations to take a lateral view of profits.
■ A fresh approach based on the concept of second order change is the vital starting point.
■ Second order change involves a reversal of assumptions from the concept of managing people to people managing.
■ The concept of sustainable development provides a useful basis for planning change.
■ Improvement starts with achieving a measure of consistency through:

— realism
— leadership by example
— ensuring contradictions can be aired
— compilation of a set of guiding principles

■ Make the easy improvements first.
■ Systematic development begins with working with people on a review of systems capability.
■ In managing standards opt for loose tolerances tightly enforced.
■ It is more important to prevent people from becoming de-motivated than to worry about what motivates them.
■ Build upon initial improvements by encouraging employees to define standards and objectives.
■ In a quality culture, all employees will need to assume managerial responsibility.
■ Organisations need to abandon current resource allocation practices and concentrate upon providing what is needed.

- Managers will need to learn new skills of resource management.
- De-skilling is counter-productive in a quality culture.
- Continuous improvement must proceed simultaneously with developing human potential. Why continue to waste resources?
- Management as we know it will eventually become redundant.
- The emphasis in a quality culture will be upon individual regulation.

REFERENCES

1 THE QUALITY MOVEMENT

1. Rickert, E (1948) *Chaucer's World*, Columbia University Press, New York, p 22.
2. Rickert, *op cit.*
3. Scherkenbach, W W (1986) *The Deming Route to Quality and Productivity*, Mercury, London, p 1.
4. Deming, E (1986) *Out of the Crisis*, Cambridge Unversity Press, Cambridge.
5. Deming, *op cit.*
6. Stalk, G Jr, and Hout, T M (1990) *Competing Against Time*, Free Press, New York.
7. Shingo, S (1988) *Non-Stock Production*, Productivity Press, Cambridge, MA.
8. *Financial Times*, 24 April, 1992.
9. Sasaki, T (1991) 'How the Japanese accelerated new car development' *Long Range Planning* 24 (1) pp 15–25.
10. Freemantle, B (1987) *The Steal*, Star, London.
11. Drummond, H and Chell, E (1992) 'Should organizations pay for quality?' *Personnel Review* 21 (2) pp 46–54.

2 THE DEMING PHILOSOPHY

1. Deming, E (1986) *Out of the Crisis*, Cambridge University Press, Cambridge. This chapter draws heavily upon this source. To avoid repetition, only specific quotations are cited.
2. Peters, T J and Waterman, R H (1982) *In Search of Excellence*, Harper & Row, New York.
3. Deming, *op cit*, p 129.
4. Scherkenbach, W W (1986) *The Deming Route to Quality and Productivity*, Mercury, London.
5. Crosby, P (1979) *Quality is Free*, McGraw-Hill, New York.

6. Morel, J (1983) *Pullman*, David & Charles, Newton Abbot, p 164.
7. Deming, *op cit*, p 51.
8. Scherkenbach, *op cit*, p 10.
9. Oakland, J S (1989) *Total Quality Management*, Heinemann, London.
10. Ayuayo, R (1990) *Dr Deming*, Mercury, London.
11. Wood, C (1988) *Boom and Bust*, Sidgwick and Jackson, London.
12. Deming, *op cit*, p 86.

3 DESIGNING FOR QUALITY

1. Taguchi, G and Clausing, D (1990) 'Robust quality' *Harvard Business Review*, January–February, p 65.
2. Taguchi, G and Wu, Y (1985) *Introduction to Off-Line Quality Control*, Central Japan Quality Control Association, Nagoya.
3. Taguchi, G (1981) *On-line Quality Control During Production*, Japanese Standards Association, Tokyo, p 7.
4. Schumacher, E F (1980) *Good Work*, Abacus, London.
5. Schonberger, R J (1982) *Japanese Manufacturing Techniques: Nine Hidden Lessons in Simplicity*, Free Press, New York.
6. Oakland, J S (1989) *Total Quality Management*, Heinemann, London.
7. Drummond, H 'Another fine mess: time for quality in decision making' *Journal of General Management* (forthcoming).
8. *Financial Times*, 4 November, 1991, p 12.
9. Drummond, H (1991) *Effective Decision Making*, Kogan Page, London.
10. Perrow, C (1984) *Normal Accidents*, Basic Books, New York.
11. Drummond (1991) *op cit*.
12. Sasaki, T (1991) 'How the Japanese accelerated new car development' *Long Range Planning* 24 (1) pp 15–25.
13. Schonberger, R J (1986) *World Class Manufacturing: The Lessons of Simplicity Applied*, Free Press, New York.
14. Pilditch, J (1989) *Winning Ways*, Mercury, London.
15. Pilditch, *op cit*.
16. Ishikawa, K (1985) *What is Total Quality Control? The Japanese Way* Prentice-Hall, Englewood Cliffs, NJ.
17. Deming, E (1986) *Out of the Crisis*, Cambridge University Press, Cambridge.
18. Schonberger (1982) *op cit*, citing Johnson p 150.
19. Deming, *op cit*.
20. Schonberger (1982) *op cit*.
21. Hayes, R and Wheelwright, S C (1984) *Restoring Our Competitive Edge*, John Wiley, New York.
22. Hayes and Wheelwright, *op cit*.
23. Williams, H (1985) *APT: A Promise Unfulfilled*, Ian Allen, London.
24. Deming *op cit*.

25. Drummond, H and Chell, E (n.d.) 'Entrepreneurial personality and sole principle solicitor's firms', Unpublished mimeo, University of Liverpool.

4 CONFORMANCE TO DESIGN

1. Crosby, P (1979) *Quality is Free*, McGraw-Hill, New York, p 19.
2. Crosby, *op cit*, p 66.
3. Department of Transport (1989) *Investigation into the Clapham Junction Railway Accident*, HMSO, London.
4. Shingo, S (1986) *Zero Quality Control: Source Inspection and the Poka-yoke System*, Productivity Press, Cambridge, MA.
5. Taguchi, G and Clausing, D (1990) 'Robust quality' *Harvard Business Review* January/February, pp 65–102.
6. See for example Lock, D and Smith, D J (1990) *Gower Handbook of Quality Management*, Gower, Aldershot.
7. Smith, D J and Edge, J 'Essential quality procedures' in *Gower Handbook of Quality Management*, p 483.
8. Smith and Edge, *op cit*, p 484.
9. See Oakland, J S (1989) *Total Quality Management*, Heinemann, London.
10. Smith and Edge, *op cit*, p 485.
11. Shingo, *op cit.*
12. Shingo, *op cit.*
13. Shingo, *op cit.*
14. Oakland, J S and Followell, R F (1990) *Statistical Process Control: A Practical Guide*, Heinemann, London.

5 QUALITY CERTIFICATION

1. British Standard BS 5750 (1979) *Quality Systems*, British Standards Institution.
2. British Standard BS 5750 (1987) *Quality Systems*. Part 1, Specification for Design Development, Production, Installation and Servicing, Section 1.1.

Note: the various sections of BS 5750 comprise:
(a) British Standard BS 5750, Part 0, Section 0.1, Guide to Selection and Use, British Standards Institution (1987).
(b) British Standard BS 5750, Part 0, Section 0.2, Guide to Quality Management and Quality System Elements, British Standards Institution (1987).
(c) British Standard BS 5750, Part 2, Specification for Production and Installation, British Standards Institution (1987).
(d) British Standard BS 5750, Part 3, Specification for Final Inspection and Test, British Standards Institution (1987).

(e) British Standard BS 5750, Part 4, Guide to the Use of BS 5750, British Standards Institution (1990).
This last is a key document, as it explains what is entailed in obtaining certification. See p 72–5.

6 QUALITY IN SERVICE ORGANISATIONS

1. Norman, R (1984) *Service Management*, John Wiley, Chichester.
2. Parasumaran, A, Zeithhalm, V, and Berry, L (1986) *Servqual; A multi-item scale for measuring customer perceptions of service quality* Marketing Science Institute, working paper report No. 86–108, August.
3. Norman, *op cit.*
4. King, C A (1987) 'A framework for a service quality assurance system' *Quality Progress*, September, pp 27–32.
5. Gronroos, C (1983) 'Innovative marketing strategies and organisation structures for service firms' in L Berry *et al* (eds), *Proceedings, Emery's Perspective on Service Marketing*, American Marketing Association, Chicago.
6. Oberoi, U and Hales, C (1990) 'Assessing the quality of the conference hotel service product: towards an empirically based model' *The Services Industries Journal* 10 (4) pp 700–21.
7. Parasumaran, *et al op cit.*
8. Edvardsson, B (1988) 'Service quality in customer relationships: A study of critical incidents in mechanical engineering companies' *The Services Industries Journal* 8 (4) pp 428–45.
9. Horovitz, J and Cudence-Poom, C (1990) 'Putting service quality into gear' *The Services Industries Journal* 10 (2) pp 249–65.
10. Sayers, D (1970) *Clouds of Witness*, New English Library, London.
11. Schlenker, B R (1980) *Impression Management*, Brooks Cole, California.
12. Prisig, R (1974) *Zen and the Art of Motorcycle Maintenance*, Corgi, London.
13. Mintzberg, H (1979) 'An emerging strategy of direct research' *Administrative Science Quarterly* 24 pp 582–9.
14. Handy, C (1990) *The Age of Unreason*, Arrow, London.

7 TIME

1. Marx, K and Engels, F (1976) *Collected Works*, Volume 6, Lawrence & Wishart, London, p 127.
2. Stalk, G Jr and Hout, T M (1990) *Competing Against Time*, Free Press, New York.
3. Shingo, S (1988) *Non-Stock Production*, Productivity Press, Cambridge, MA.
4. Stalk and Hout *op cit.*
5. Shingo, S (1989) *A Study of the Toyota Production System*, Productivity Press, Cambridge, MA.
6. Shingo, S (1987) *The Sayings of Shigeo Shingo: Key Strategies for Plant Improvement*, Productivity Press, Cambridge, MA.
7. Ohno, T with Mito, S (1988) *Just-In-Time for Today and Tomorrow*, Productivity Press, Cambridge, MA.

8. Shingo (1988) *op cit.*
9. Pike, A (1992) 'A speedy recovery' *Financial Times*, 7 February, p 10.
10. Shingo (1988) *op cit.*
11. Schonberger, R J (1982) *Japanese Manufacturing Techniques: Nine Hidden Lessons in Simplicity*, Free Press, New York, p 16.
12. Ohno, T (1984) 'How the Toyota production system was created' in Sato, K and Hoshino, Y (eds) *The Anatomy of Japanese Business*, M E Sharpe, New York.
13. Stalk and Hout *op cit.*
14. Deming, E (1986) *Out of the Crisis*, Cambridge University Press, Cambridge.
15. Rainnie, A (1991) 'Just-in-time, sub-contracting and the small firm' *Work Employment and Society* 5 (3) pp 353–75.
16. Turnbull, P J (1988) 'The limits to "Japanization" – Just-in-time, labour relations and the UK automative industry' *New Technology Work and Employment* 31 Spring pp 7–20.
17. Tomaney, J (1990) 'The reality of workplace flexibility' *Capital and Class* 40 Spring pp 29–60.
18. Dawson, P and Webb, J (1989) 'New production arrangements: the totally flexible cage?' *Work Employment and Society* 3 (2) pp 221–38.
19. Turnbull *op cit.*

8 BUILDING A QUALITY CULTURE

1. Nyerere, J (1973) *Freedom and Development*, Oxford, Dares Salaam. (I am indebted to Marylin Wood a former Liverpool M.B.A. student for access to this quotation.)
2. Hutchins, D (1985) *Quality Circles Handbook*, Pitman, London, p 3.
3. Hill, S (1991) 'Why quality circles failed but Total Quality might succeed,' *British Journal of Industrial Relations* (29).
4. Klaus, R and Bass, B M (1974) 'Group influence on individual behaviour across cultures' *Journal of Cross Cultural Psychology*, 5, pp 236–46.
5. Naoi, A and Schooler, C (1985) 'Occupational conditions and psychological functioning in Japan' *American Journal of Sociology*, 90(4), pp 729–52.
6. Hofstede, G (1980) *Culture's Consequences: International Differences in Work Related Values*, Sage, Beverley Hills.
7. Lincoln, J R, Hanada, M and Olsen, J (1981) 'Cultural orientations and individual reactions to organizations: a study of employees of Japanese-owned firms,' *Administrative Science Quarterly*, 26, pp 93–115.
8. Luthans, E, McCaul, H S and Dodd, N G (1985) 'Organizational commitment, a comparison of American, Japanese and Korean employees', *Academy of Management Journal*, 23(1), 213–19.
9. Watzlawick, P, Weakland, J H and Fisch, R (1974) *Change: Principles of Problem Formation and Resolution*, Norton, New York.
10. Hawkins, S (1988) *A Brief History of Time*, Bantam Press, London.
11. Lewis, M (1990) *Liar's Poker*, Coronet, London.

12. Peters, T J and Waterman, R H (1982) *In Search of Excellence*, Harper & Row, New York.
13. Thompson, E P (1967) 'Time, work-discipline and industrial capitalism' *Past and Present*, 38, pp 56–97.
14. Zipkin, P H (1991) 'Does manufacturing need a JIT revolution?' *Harvard Business Review*, January/February, pp 40–52.
15. Dawson, P and Webb, J (1989) 'New production arrangements: the totally flexible cage?' *Work Employment and Society*, 3(2), pp 221–38.
16. Wall, T D, Corbett, R M, Clegg, C W and Jackson, P R (1990) 'Advanced manufacturing technology, work design, and performance: A change study' *Journal of Applied Psychology*, 75(6), 691–97.

A GUIDE TO FURTHER READING

GENERAL

The best overall guide to TQM philosophy is **Deming's** *Out of the Crisis*. It is lengthy and repetitive in places but is clear, readable and entertaining. Works about the Deming approach tend to repeat Deming's ideas.

Crosby's *Quality is Free* is a lively and entertaining introduction to TQM and is available in a very cheap paperback edition. Crosby tends to emphasise the conformance aspects of quality and is shallow on implementation, relying largely upon 'hype'. Later works are mainly more of the same. Similar comments apply to the various works of **Peters** and **Waterman** – inspirational but undisciplined.

For an analytical approach to the subject see **Garvin's** *Managing Quality*. For strategic issues see the various publications of **Hayes** *et al*, and **Schonberger**. Bear in mind that some of Schonberger's accounts of Japanese practice are screened.

A good source of information on all aspects of quality is the *Harvard Business Review*. The *Sloan Management Review* also carries frequent articles, particularly on the strategic aspects of quality.

THE SERVICE INDUSTRIES

Martin's *'Restaurant Manager's Bible,'* encapsulates the spirit of quality in service organisations. **Norman's** book *Service Management* provides a more systematic approach and is the touchstone of many later works and research.

Research is developing rapidly; see *The Service Industries Journal* for reports of developments.

TECHNICAL ASPECTS OF QUALITY

Juran and **Feigenbaum** are authorities. Works by Japanese authors notably **Shingo, Monden, Ohno** and **Taguchi** are well worth consulting but hard going, partly because the texts are extremely dense and detailed, and partly because they are rich in profound insights typically expressed in single sentences. The mathematics of Taguchi need not delay the general reader – for a critical commentary see **Box** *et al.*

PROCEDURAL ASPECTS OF QUALITY

Oakland's *Total Quality Management* combines an introduction to TQM philosophy with a systematic blue print for action. Detailed analysis of the issues of costing and technical management of quality is contained in works by **Dale** and **Plunkett.** The *Gower Handbook* edited by **Lock** and **Smith** is less rigorous but contains useful guidance on the practicalities of writing quality manuals and the like.

STATISTICAL PROCESS CONTROL

Oakland and **Followell's** *Statistical Process Control* is both comprehensive and comprehensible by the non-numerate reader. **Deming's** *Out of the Crisis* also contains a lucid explanation.

ORGANISATIONAL ISSUES

For a non-academic insight into the meaning of alienation see **Prisig,** *Zen and the Art of Motorcycle Maintenance.* **Schumacher's** *Good Work* and *Small is Beautiful* are both relevant to concepts of work and organisation. See **Handy's** *Age of Unreason* for a futuristic perspective on both of these concepts. **Baverman's** *Labour and Monopoly Capital* contains a fascinating analysis of the impact of Taylorism. **Knight's** *et al* provides useful insights into the employee relations implications of bonus schemes and organisation for production. **Holloway** gives access to the historical development of human resource management.

The leading journals on the political aspects of management include *The British Journal of Industrial Relations, Capital and Class, The Journal of Industrial Relations* and *Work Employment and Society.*

BIBLIOGRAPHY

Baverman, H (1974) *Labour and Monopoly Capital*, Monthly Review Press, New York.

Box, G, Bisgaard, S and Fung, C (1988) 'An explanation and critique of Taguchi's contributions to quality engineering' *Quality and Reliability Engineering International* 4, pp 123–31.

Dale, B and Plunkett, G (1989) *Managing Quality*, Philip Allen, London.

Dale, B and Plunkett, G (1991) *Quality Costing*, Chapman & Hall, London.

Deming, E (1986) *Out of the Crisis*, Cambridge University Press, Cambridge.

Feigenbaum, A V (1961, 1963), *Total Quality Control*, McGraw-Hill, New York.

Garvin, D A (1988) *Managing Quality*, Free Press, New York.

Hayes, R and Wheelwright, S C (1984) *Restoring Our Competitive Edge*, John Wiley, New York.

Hayes, R, Wheelwright, S C and Clark, K B (1988) *Dynamic Manufacturing*, Free Press, New York.

Handy, C (1990) *The Age of Unreason*, Arrow, London.

Holloway, W (1991) *Work Psychology and Organizational Behaviour*, Sage, London.

Juran, J M (1974) *Quality Control Handbook*, McGraw-Hill, New York.

Juran, J M and Gryana, F M (1980) *Quality Planning and Analysis*, McGraw-Hill, New York.

Juran, J M (1988) *Juran on Planning for Quality*, Free Press, New York.

Knights, D, Willmot, H and Collinson, D (Eds) (1985) *Job Redesign*, Gower, Aldershot.

Lock, D and Smith, D J (1990) *Gower Handbook of Quality Management*, Gower, Aldershot.

Martin, W B (1986) *Quality Service: The Restaurant Manager's Bible*, Ithaca, Cornell University, New York.

Monden, Y (1983) *Toyota Production System: Practical Approach to Production Management*, Norcross, GA, Management Press, Institute of Industrial Engineers.

Norman, R (1984) *Service Management*, John Wiley, Chichester.

Oakland, J S (1989) *Total Quality Management*, Heinemann, London.

Oakland, J S and Followell, R F (1990) *Statistical Process Control: A Practical Guide*, Heinemann, London.

Ohno, T (1984) 'How the Toyota production system was created,' in Sato, K and Hoshino, Y (Eds) (1984) *The Anatomy of Japanese Business*, M E Sharpe, New York.

Ohno, T, with Mito, S (1988) *Just-in-Time for Today and Tomorrow*, Productivity Press, Cambridge, MA.

Ohno, T (1988) *Toyota Production System: Beyond Large Scale Production*, Productivity Press, Cambridge, MA.

Peters, T J and Waterman, R H (1982) *In Search of Excellence*, Harper & Row, New York.

Peters, T J and Austin, N (1985) *A Passion For Excellence*, Random House, New York.

Peters, T (1988) *Thriving on Chaos*, Alfred A Knopf, New York.

Prisig, R (1974) *Zen and the Art of Motorcycle Maintenance*, Corgi, London.

Shingo, S (1985) *A Revolution in Manufacturing*, Productivity Press, Cambridge, MA.

Shingo, S (1986) *Zero Quality Control: Source Inspection and the Poka-yoke System*. Productivity Press, Cambridge, MA.

Shingo, S (1987) *The Sayings of Shigeo Shingo: Key Strategies for Plant Improvement*, Productivity Press, Cambridge, MA.

Shingo, S (1988) *Non-Stock Production*, Productivity Press, Cambridge, MA.

Shingo, S (1989) *A Study of the Toyota Production System*, Productivity Press, Cambridge, MA.

Schonberger, R J (1982), *Japanese Manufacturing Techniques: Nine Hidden Lessons in Simplicity*, Free Press, New York.

Schonberger, R J (1986) *World Class Manufacturing: The Lessons of Simplicity Applied*, Free Press, New York.

Schonberger, R J (1990) *Building a Chain of Customers: Linking Business Functions to Create a World Class Company*, Free Press, New York.

Schumacher, E F (1976) *Small is Beautiful*, Abacus, London.

Schumacher, E F (1980) *Good Work*, Abacus, London.

Waterman, H Jr (1987) *The Renewal Factor*, Bantam, London.

INDEX